Brilliant Computing for the Over 50s

Over 50s

Microsoft ® Windows 7 edition

P.K. MacBride

Prentice Hall
is an imprint of

Harlow, England • London • New York • Boston • San Francisco • Toronto • Sydney • Singapore • Hong Kong
Tokyo • Seoul • Taipei • New Delhi • Cape Town • Madrid • Mexico City • Amsterdam • Munich • Paris • Milan

Pearson Education Limited
Edinburgh Gate
Harlow
Essex CM20 2JE
England

and Associated Companies throughout the world

Visit us on the World Wide Web at:
www.pearsoned.co.uk

First published 2006
Second edition published 2007
Third edition published 2009

© Pearson Education Limited 2006, 2009

ISBN: 978-0-273-73055-2

British Library Cataloguing-in-Publication Data
A catalogue record for this book is available from the British Library

Library of Congress Cataloging-in-Publication Data
A CIP catalog record for this book can be obtained from the Library of Congress

10 9 8 7 6 5 4 3 2 1
13 12 11 10 09

Prepared for Pearson Education Ltd by Syllaba Ltd (http://www.syllaba.co.uk).
Typeset in 11pt Arial Condensed by 30
Printed and bound in Great Britain by Ashford Colour Press Ltd, Gosport, Hants.

The publisher's policy is to use paper manufactured from sustainable forests.

Brilliant guides

What you need to know and how to do it

When you're working on your computer and come up against a problem that you're unsure how to solve, or want to accomplish something that you aren't sure how to do, where do you look? Manuals and traditional training guides are usually too big and unwieldy and are intended to be used as end-to-end training resources, making it hard to get to the info you need right away without having to wade through pages of background information that you just don't need at that moment – and helplines are rarely that helpful!

Brilliant guides have been developed to allow you to find the info you need easily and without fuss and guide you through the task using a highly visual, step-by-step approach – providing exactly what you need to know when you need it!

Brilliant guides provide the quick easy-to-access information that you need, using a table of contents and troubleshooting guide to help you find exactly what you need to know, and then presenting each task in a visual manner. Numbered steps guide you through each task or problem, using numerous screenshots to illustrate each step. Added features include 'See also' boxes that point you to related tasks and information in the book, while 'Did you know?' sections alert you to relevant expert tips, tricks and advice to further expand your skills and knowledge.

In addition to covering all major office PC applications, and related computing subjects, the *Brilliant* series also contains titles that will help you in every aspect of your working life, such as writing the perfect CV, answering the toughest interview questions and moving on in your career.

Brilliant guides are the light at the end of the tunnel when you are faced with any minor or major task.

Publisher's acknowledgements

The author and publisher would like to thank the following for permission to reproduce the screen shots in this book:

Yahoo! UK, Google UK, Saga, Real and Yamaha Motor Co.

Microsoft product screen shots reprinted with permission from Microsoft Corporation. FujiFilm screen shots reprinted with permission from FujiFilm Electronic Imaging Ltd.

Every effort has been made to obtain necessary permission with reference to copyright material. In some instances we have been unable to trace the owners of copyright material, and we would appreciate any information that would enable us to do so.

Author's acknowledgements

The author would like to thank Karen, Sally, Catherine and Anna for making this project so enjoyable.

About the author

P.K. MacBride spent 20 years at the chalkface in schools and technical colleges before leaving to work full-time as a writer, editor and typesetter. He has written over 100 books, mainly on computing topics, covering many aspects of computer programming, software applications and the Internet. He has been translated into over a dozen languages, including Russian, Portugese, Greek, Chinese and American.

Contents

Preface

The basic unit of computer memory is called a byte, but computers don't bite. And you can't do much damage to them either, whatever you do wrong – short of taking a hammer to them. The worst that can normally happen is that it will stop working, half-way through a job and that's easily solved – just turn it off and on again. For the most part, computer systems are logical, work in standard ways and follow the same set of basic rules. Once you understand those rules, you will be able to use your computer effectively, and tackle new applications confidently. This book will show you those rules. So, shed your fears. You can't break it, and it won't break you.

Being over 50 is no handicap when it comes to learning about computers. I'm over 50, though I've been using computers for 20-odd years, but I have many friends and relations who have come to computers, and mastered them, in their 50s, 60s, 70s and even 80s. We can all learn new things at any age. The biggest bar to learning is the belief that it will be difficult. Relax, using a computer is not difficult. (Designing a computer or developing new computer applications are, but no-one is asking you to do these things!)

Being over 50 may well, however, affect the sort of things that you want to learn about computers. If I had been writing this book for the under 50s, I would have included chapters on the full range of office applications: word processing, spreadsheets, databases and presentation software, because younger people may well need these to take their careers forward. Us older folks, if we are still in work, probably have all the IT skills we need for the job, and if we are now starting to learn about computers, it is for use in our leisure activities. We want to use them to write letters, minutes of meetings or our memoirs; create newsletters and posters for our clubs, store, edit, organise and print our digital photos and videos; get online and explore the internet. And that's what this book is about.

There are several different types of computer around, and lots of software. This book is for people who have a PC (desktop or laptop of any make) running Windows 7, perhaps with Word or Works as the word-processor. Apart from that, all the software that is covered in this book is supplied as part of the Windows 7 package, or can be downloaded, free of charge, from Microsoft's Windows Live site. That software is all that most of us need.

P.K. MacBride, Southampton 2009

Introduction

i

Welcome to *Brilliant Computing for the Over 50s, Windows 7 edition,* a visual quick reference book that shows you how to make the most of your PC. Focused specifically on the needs of those whose working life was not affected significantly by computers, it provides an introductory guide to using a computer. It will show you how to work in the Windows environment, organise your files, use a word processor, store and edit images from a camera, configure Windows to suit you, and will start you off exploring the Internet and communicating by email.

Find what you need to know – when you need it

You don't have to read this book in any particular order. We've designed the book so that you can jump in, get the information you need, and jump out. To find the information that you need, just look up the task in the table of contents or Troubleshooting guide, and turn to the page listed. Read the task introduction, follow the step-by-step instructions along with the illustration, and you're done.

How this book works

Each task is presented with step-by-step instructions in one column and screen illustrations in the other. This arrangement lets you focus on a single task without having to turn the pages too often.

How you'll learn

Find what you need to know – when you need it

How this book works

Step-by-step instructions

Troubleshooting guide

Spelling

Step-by-step instructions

This book provides concise step-by-step instructions that show you how to accomplish a task. Each set of instructions includes illustrations that directly correspond to the easy-to-read steps. Eye-catching text features provide additional helpful information in bite-sized chunks to help you work more efficiently or to teach you more in-depth information. The 'For your information' feature provides tips and techniques to help you work smarter, while the 'See also' cross-references lead you to other parts of the book containing related information about the task. Essential information is highlighted in 'Important' boxes that will ensure you don't miss any vital suggestions and advice.

Troubleshooting guide

This book offers quick and easy ways to diagnose and solve common problems that you might encounter using the Troubleshooting guide. The problems are grouped into categories that are presented alphabetically.

Spelling

We have used UK spelling conventions throughout this book. You may therefore notice some inconsistencies between the text and the software on your computer which is likely to have been developed in the USA. We have however adopted US spelling for the words 'disk' and 'program' as these are becoming commonly accepted throughout the world.

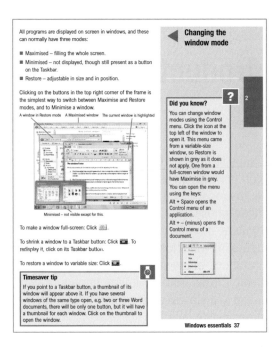

Instant computing

1

Introduction

Computing does not have to be difficult. You don't need a degree in Computer Science to produce a letter or the minutes of a meeting with a word processor, or to draw a picture or diagram on the screen. (Of course, you do need a degree in Computer Science, or something like it, if you are going to develop new software or design new equipment, but that's not what we're about here!) In this first chapter you will see how little you need to learn to be able to do useful things with your computer. We will explore three applications that are present in every Windows 7 computer:

- WordPad, a simple but effective word processor
- Windows Explorer, which is used for managing files
- Paint, a basic application for creating and editing images.

> ## ! Important
>
> Windows 7 allows its users to customise the screen in many ways. As a result, your screen may well not look exactly the same as the ones in the screenshots. You will see how to customise the display in Chapter 9.

Discovering your PC

A desktop PC system typically has these components:

Monitor or VDU (Visual Display Unit). On older desktop PCs this is similar to a TV, but most now have flat LCD screens. Newer monitors usually have 17-inch screens, capable of resolutions up to 1,600 × 1,200. (The resolution is the number of pixels – dots of light – that make up the screen.)

System unit – the box containing the 'works'. This may act as a base for the monitor, or stand beside it, as in the illustration, or on the floor beneath.

On the front you should be able to see the front panels of a floppy disk drive and a CD/DVD-ROM drive, and two buttons – one is the on/off button, the other the reset button.

At the back you will find a number of sockets and connections, most with cables plugged into them.

Inside, and best left to the experts, are the power supply, the CD/DVD-ROM, floppy disk and hard disk drives, and the main circuit board (the motherboard) containing the main processor, the memory and other chips; plus a sound card, graphics card, modem and other circuit boards.

Keyboard – though mainly for entering text and numbers, the keys can also be used for controlling software, as you will see.

Mouse – used for controlling the cursor on screen, allowing you to select items, start programs, draw pictures, and more.

There will also normally be speakers and a printer, and possibly a scanner, attached.

For your information

A portable or laptop PC is in practice the same as a desktop model, except that the screen is in the lid and the system unit is in the base of the keyboard. There will usually be some form of touch pad or mini-joystick in the keyboard to use in place of a mouse.

Windows is an operating system – and more. An operating system handles the interaction between the processor and the screen, memory, mouse, disk drives, printer and other equipment. It is a bridge between the hardware of the computer and the applications – such as word processing or spreadsheet programs. Whatever hardware you are using, if it has a version of Windows, it can run any application written for that or for earlier versions of Windows. (This book assumes that you are using Windows 7 – but if you have an earlier version, such as Vista, the differences are not very great.)

Start up

1 Turn on the PC.

2 If the monitor has its own switch, turn it on.

3 Various messages and images will appear to let you know that things are happening.

4 If you are on a network, you will need to log on – to enter your user name and password.

5 After a few more minutes' wait while the last files are loaded and the system configured for your use, the Desktop screen will appear.

rtcuts   Ribbon   Menu bar   Program windows   Desktop   Gadgets

Start button   Taskbar   Clock

Shortcuts – instant access to programs. You can create shortcuts.
Menu bar – gives access to a program's commands.
Ribbon – another way to access a program's commands.
Desktop – you can change the background picture or pattern and its colours.
Program windows – adjust their size and placing to suit yourself.
Start button – opens the Start menu, from where you should be able to start any program on your PC.
Taskbar – when a program is running, it has a button here. Click on a button to open its window and bring it to the front of the desktop.
Clock – optional, but handy.

Starting a program

The programs already on your PC, and any that you install later will have an entry somewhere on the Start menu. Those that you use most often are listed on the left-hand side, ready for a quick start. All the rest can be reached through the All Programs part of the menu.

A program can also be started by selecting a document or file that was created by it. Those that you have been working on recently are also present on the Start menu. Click on one of these links to start the program and open the document, ready for work.

Starting a program

1 Click the Start button.

2 If the program is listed, click on its name.

or

3 Point to All programs.

4 If necessary, click on the folder that contains the program.

5 Click on the program's name.

Starting from a document.

1 Click the Start button.

2 Point to the program with which you created the document.

3 Click on the document.

4

Word processing is one of the most popular uses of computers, and not surprising. Word processing puts well presented, neatly formatted, correctly spelled documents in the reach of everyone.

Windows 7 comes with its own word processor – WordPad. This does not have the full scope of a professional package, such as Word, but it has a good range of formatting facilities. You can set selected text in any font, size or colour, add emphasis with **bold**, *italics* and <u>underline</u>, indent paragraphs or set their alignment, and even insert pictures, clip art, charts and many other types of objects. WordPad has all you need for writing letters, essays, memos, reports and the like. Could you write a book on it? Possibly, as long as it had a simple layout and you were happy to create the contents list and index by hand.

Most of us, most of the time, use only a fraction of the facilities of full-blown word processors. It is often more efficient to use WordPad – because it is simpler, faster to load and to run, and faster to learn!

Start WordPad

1 Click the Start button.

2 Point to All Programs.

3 Click on the Accessories folder.

4 Click on WordPad.

! Important

The best way to learn is to play. As you read through the next few pages, use WordPad to write a letter, or make notes on what you are learning, or even start that novel! But don't take it seriously. Keep the focus on exploring WordPad, not on the content of the document.

▶

Starting word processing (cont.)

Entering text

All word-processors have word wrap. Don't press Enter as you get close to the right margin. WordPad will sense when a word is going to go over the end of a line and wrap it round to the start of the next. The only time you should press Enter is at the end of a paragraph or to create a blank line. If you change the margins of the page or the size of the font, WordPad will shuffle the text to fit, word wrapping as it goes.

Selecting text

- A block of text – anything from a single character to the whole document – is selected when it is highlighted. Once selected the text can be formatted, copied, deleted or moved.

- The simplest way to select text is to drag the mouse pointer over it. Take care if some of the text is below the visible area, as the scrolling can run away with you!

- A good alternative is to click the insertion point into place at the start of the block you want to select, then hold down Shift and use the arrow keys to move the highlight to the end of the block.

- When setting alignment or indents, which can only apply to whole paragraphs, it is enough to place the insertion point – the flashing vertical line where you type – into the paragraph.

- Double-click anywhere in a word to select it.

- Triple-click anywhere in a paragraph to select it.

Deleting errors

To correct mistakes, press Backspace to remove the last character you typed, or select the unwanted text and press either Backspace or Delete.

Important

One of the great things about Windows applications – especially those from Microsoft – is that they do the same jobs in the same way. Once you have learnt how to enter text, open or save a file, select a font or whatever, in one application, you will know how to do it in the next.

You can do formatting in two ways – either select existing text and apply the format to it, or set up the format and then start typing. Either way, the formats are selected in the same way.

Use the options in the Font part of the Ribbon to change aspects of the formatting – just click on the appropriate button or select from the drop-down lists.

If you have selected some existing text, when you scroll down the Font list, the text on screen will be displayed in the font that you are pointing to – this is known as Live Preview. The font will not actually change until you click on one in the list. When you find the one you want, click on the name. The Font Size list also gives you the same Live Preview.

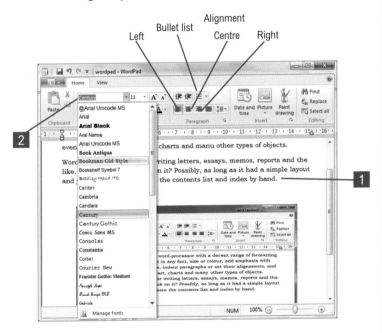

Left / Bullet list / Alignment / Centre / Right

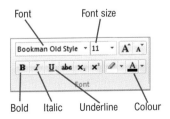

Font / Font size / Bold / Italic / Underline / Colour

1 Select the text or go to where the new format is to start.

2 Use the Formatting tools.

Click on a button to apply or remove its formatting.

Or click the arrow beside the button to display its options and select one from the list or palette.

Important

In WordPad, as in most new applications from Microsoft, the commands are selected from the Ribbon – the strip that runs across the top of the workspace. This has two tabs, 'Home' and 'View'. Click on the tab name to bring its set of commands to the front. Within each tab, the commands are held in groups. To use a command, either click on its button, or click on its arrow to open a set of options.

Formatting paragraphs

The formatting options in the Font group can be applied to any amount of text, from a single character to the whole document. The options in the Paragraph group can only be applied to complete paragraphs. Use these to set the alignment of the text between the margins, to add bullets, increase or reduce the indent (the distance in from the left margin) and set the line spacing.

1 Select the paragraph(s) – and note that a paragraph is selected if the cursor is in it, or if any part of it is highlighted.

2 Click on a button to apply its formatting.

or

3 With the Bullets or Line Spacing buttons, click on the arrow to open a set of options, and select from there.

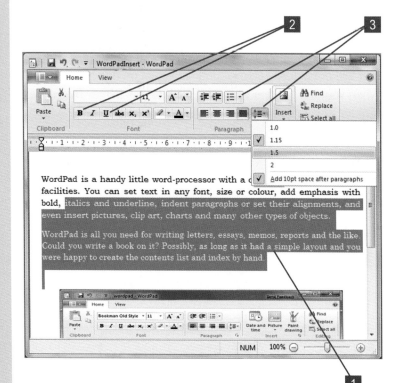

Anything you type into WordPad – or most other applications – is lost when you close the application unless you save the document as a file on a disk.

The first time that you save a file, you have to specify where to put it and what to call it. If you then edit it and want to store it again, you can use File, Save to resave it with the same name in the same place, overwriting the old file. If you edit a file and want to keep the old copy and the new one, then you can use File, Save As and save the new version under a different name.

In WordPad – again, as in many applications – you can save a file in several ways. The default is Rich Text Format, which can be read by most word processors and many other applications. You can also save the words, without the formatting, by using one of the text formats.

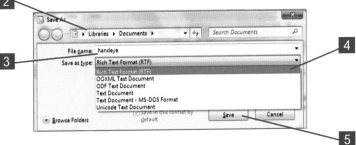

To save a new file

1. Click the WordPad button (at the top left) and select Save As from the main menu.

2. The top left slot shows the folder that the file will be saved in. You can change this, but we won't bother with changing folders at this stage.

3. Type in a name to identify the file clearly.

4. Change the Save as type if necessary.

5. Click Save.

Resaving a file

6. Click the Save icon in the Quick Access Toolbar at the top of the window.

Important

If you open a Word document in WordPad, you can save it again in Word format.

Closing and reopening files

Once a document has been saved as a file it can be reopened again whenever you want to add to it or edit it, or print out another copy. Just to prove this, we'll close the document – and close WordPad for good measure – then reopen it.

Close a file

1 Open the main menu and select New. (You will then need to select the type of document – choose Rich Text Format.) The current file will be closed – you may be prompted to save it.

Shut down WordPad

2 Open the main menu and select Exit or click [×].

Restart WordPad

3 Click the Start button.

4 Point to All Programs.

5 Point to the Accessories folder.

6 Click on WordPad.

Open the file

7 Open the main menu and select Open.

8 Locate and select your file.

9 Click Open.

In almost every Windows application there are two ways to print a document:

Use the Quick Print command to print one copy of the whole document, using the default printer. (You can add a Quick Print icon to the Quick Access toolbar, for faster printing.)

Open the Print dialogue box to print selected pages, or set the number of copies, or control the quality of the printing.

Here's how printing works in WordPad. Use it to print your new file.

◀ Printing a document

1

Quick Print

1 Check that the printer is on and that there is paper in it.

2 Open the main menu, point to Print and select Quick Print.

Control the printout

1 If you only want to print part of the document, select it now.

2 Open the main menu, point to Print and select Print.

3 If you have a choice, select the printer.

4 In the Page Range area, choose what to print: the entire document, the part you selected earlier or a set of pages (type the number for a single page, or the first and last numbers, e.g. 3–5).

5 If you want more than one copy, enter how many.

6 Click Print.

Timesaver tip

If you only want the printout for your reference, click the Preference button to open a dialogue box where you can control the quality of the printing. Set it to Draft and the document will be printed about twice as fast as usual – and it will use less ink!

Managing files

Windows Explorer (or just Explorer for short) is the tool that we use for managing the files on our disks. You can start Explorer from Computer, Documents, Pictures and several other links on the Start menu – each opens Explorer at a different part of your system.

Click the Pictures or Documents button.

Current Folder   Contents pane   Search box

Toolbar

Navigation pane

Details pane

Status bar   Preview pane

The Explorer display is highly variable. Some elements can be turned on or off, and some change in response to the material that is currently displayed. These are always present:

- The Current Folder box shows you where you are now.

- The Search box can be used to hunt for a file (see page 156).

- The Toolbar buttons vary according to what sort of folder is displayed, and what sort of file, if any, is selected at the time.

- The Contents pane usually shows the files and folders in the current folder, though for Computer it shows the disks and other storage on the PC.

These are optional, though the first two are normally present:

- The Navigation pane offers several ways to reach the files on your system: Favourites has quick links to your most used folders; Libraries groups your documents in a variety of ways; Homegroup and Network both have links to other computers on your local network (if present); and Computer lists the drives on your PC.

- The Details pane tells you the size, date and other details about the selected file or folder.

- The Preview pane shows a small version of an image or the first page of other documents, if a preview is available.

- The Search pane opens up when you run an advanced search.

- The Menu bar gives another way to reach the commands and options. Compared to the selected and context-sensitive Toolbar, which changes as you work, this has the advantage that every command is always there, and in the same place.

You will see later (page 130) how to turn these elements on and off.

The Toolbar contents vary, depending upon the file selected. These buttons are always or often there:

Organize ▼	Shows a menu of commands for managing files.
Print	Prints one copy of the selected file.
Open ▼	Opens the selected file for reading or editing.
Share with	Controls who can have access to the file.
Burn	Copies the selected file(s) to a CD or DVD.
🔲 ▼	Views – gives you different ways to look at what's in your system.
🔲	Preview pane display – click to toggle the pane on or off.

Explore your system

1 In the Navigation pane, ▷ to the left shows that a drive or folder contains a lower level of folders.

2 Click ▷ to bring the next level of folders into view. The icon changes to ◢.

3 Click ◢ when you want to hide the lower levels of folders again.

4 Click on a folder name to select it and to list its files and folders in the main part of the display.

Using Paint

There are essentially two ways to draw an image on a computer. The picture can be made up of lines, circles, shapes, text notes, etc. each of which remains separate and can be moved, deleted, recoloured or resized at any point. This is the approach used in the drawing routine in Microsoft Word.

Paint is the graphics software that comes with Windows. It uses the alternative approach. Here the image is produced by applying colour to a background, with each new line overwriting anything that may be beneath. Using this type of graphics software is very like real painting. You can wipe out a mistake while the paint is still wet, but as soon as it has dried it is fixed on the canvas – though Paint allows you to undo the last move.

Start Paint

1 Click the Start button to open the Start menu.

2 Point to All Programs to open the list of programs. Open the Accessories folder.

3 In the Accessories menu, click on Paint.

Important

Remember that you've got to use it if you want to learn it! Run Paint and practise the techniques that are covered in these next few pages. You can easily rub out your mistakes, or if it is a real mess, start again from scratch. (Open the main menu and select New to restart.)

Paint can easily be used to produce simple diagrams, or to edit images captured from the screen.

The gridlines are there to help you draw more accurately, and will not be shown in the image file. If you do not want them, go to the View tab and turn them off.

See also

You can find out more about drawing in Word in Chapter 7.

The Toolbox

There is a simple but adequate set of tools. A little experimentation will show how they all work. Play with them! Release your inner Picasso! The notes here and on the next page may help.

Pencil Fill with colour Text Rectangle, Oval, Line, Curve, Polygon

Eraser Magnifier Brush
Airbrush

Pick colour

If a tool's button has an arrow on it, click it to see the options. Ones to note are:

- Select – rectangular or free-form area; Transparent allows you to move or copy an item without its background.
- Rotate – three directions, and two 'Flip' (mirror) options
- Brush – choose the style
- Shapes – include lines and curves (see page 16)
- Outline and Fill – only active after you have drawn a shape, and while it is still selected
- Size – sets the width of the pencil, erase or brush

Did you know?

If you hold down Shift when drawing, it makes ovals into circles; rectangles into squares and only allows lines to be drawn at 0°, 45° and 90°.

To use the Eraser, Pencil or Brush: click to leave a dot or a blob; drag for continuous drawing.

To draw a line: select Line in the Shapes set, then click where the line is to start and drag the end into position. While the line is still selected, you can drag the end into a new position, or change the size or colour.

To draw any other shape: select the type of shape, then imagine a rectangle that would enclose it and click at one corner of this and drag across to the opposite corner. While the shape is still selected, you can:

- Drag the handles at the corners or mid-sides to resize it
- Change its line thickness with the Size options
- Set the Outline or Fill options
- Pick new colours for the stroke or fill.

Drawing a curve

The curved line tool is a bit trickier than the rest. Even when you have the hang of how this works, it will still take you several goes to get a line right!

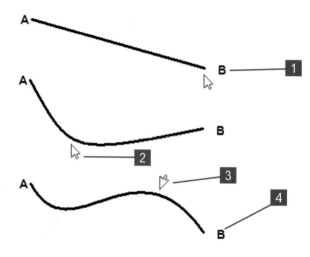

1 Draw a line between the points where the curve will start and end.

2 Click or drag to create the first curve – exaggerate the curve as it will be reduced at the next stage.

3 Drag out the second curve now – as long as the mouse button is down, the line will flex to follow the cursor.

or

4 For a single curve, just click at the end of the line.

5 While the curve is still selected, you can drag on the handles of the enclosing rectangle to change its overall size and proportions. You can also change the thickness and colour of the line.

Timesaver tip

Press Prt Sc to copy the whole screen to the Clipboard, or Alt + Prt Sc to copy the active window. The image can be pasted into Paint and saved. That's how the screenshots were produced for this book.

The colour palette is used in almost the same way in all Windows programs. You can select a colour from the palette – use the left button for the foreground colour and the right button for the background – or mix your own. Remember that you are mixing light, not paint. This means:

- red and green make yellow
- green and blue make cyan
- blue and red make magenta
- red, green and blue make white.

The more light you use, the lighter the colour.

1 Double-click on a colour in the palette or use Colours, Edit Colours.

2 At the Edit Colours dialogue box, click on a Basic or Custom Colour and go to Step 6.

or

3 Click Define Custom Colours to open the full box.

4 Drag the cross-hair cursor in the main square to set the Red/Green/Blue balance, and move the arrow up or down the scale to set the light/dark level.

5 Click Add to Custom Colours if you want to add this to the set.

6 Click OK – the new colour will replace the one currently selected in the palette on the main screen.

Did you know?

If you hold down the right mouse button, lines are drawn in the background colour instead of the foreground colour.

If you hold the button down while using the eraser, it replaces any current foreground colour with background colour.

Saving an image

If you want to keep your image, or use it in another application, you need to save it as a file. The process is very similar to saving a document in WordPad.

To save a new file

1 Open the main menu and select Save As…

2 Images are normally saved as PNG files. To use another format, select it from the list or use the 'Other formats' option.

3 Type in a File name to identify the file clearly.

4 Click Save.

The file will probably be saved in the Pictures folder. You will learn more about folders in Chapter 6.

To resave a file

5 Open the main menu and select Save.

Did you know? ?

Paint can save images in half a dozen different file formats, but the default PNG does the job very nicely for our purposes just now.

Word processors can handle other things as well as text. Even WordPad, which is probably the simplest word processor around, can cope with images. Try it now. Insert the image that you just created into your text file.

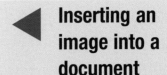

Inserting an image into a document

Insert an image

1 Run WordPad if it is not already open (see page 5).

2 Open the file you created earlier.

3 Click into the document at the point where you want to place the image.

4 Click the Picture button in the Insert group on the Ribbon.

Inserting an image into a document (cont.)

5 Select the image file.

6 Click Open.

7 The image may well not be the right size. You can change the size by dragging on the 'handles' – the little black squares – on the corners or mid-sides.

8 Save the file if you want to keep this copy with its image.

! Important

You can use the alignment buttons to change the position of an image across the width of the page. Click on the image to select it, then click the Left, Centre or Right button to set the alignment.

When you have finished work on your computer, you must shut it down properly, and not just turn it off. During a working session, application programs and Windows 7 may have created temporary files, and any data files that you have been editing may still be open in memory and not yet written safely to disk. A proper shut down closes and stores open files and removes unwanted ones.

1 Click the Start button, then click the Shut down button on the bottom right of the menu. If any windows are open, they will be closed, and you may be prompted to save documents.

or

2 Hold down Alt and press F4. If any windows are open, this will close the topmost one. Repeat to close all open windows, then press Alt + F4 again to shut down.

Important

On some laptop keyboards, you may need to hold down the Fn button, with Alt and F4, to shut down applications and the computer.

Shutting down (cont.)

Other endings

If you share the PC with other people, or want to stop work for a short while, there may be five or six options on the Shut Down menu which can end a session temporarily.

- ■ Switch User suspends your programs, and allows another user to log in. The documents that you were working on will not be affected by anything they do. When they are finished you can log in again and pick up where you left off.

- ■ Log Off ends the programs that you have been using, but leaves the PC running, for another person to use. This is the best choice if you have finished with the PC for some time, but others will want it.

- ■ Lock suspends your programs and switches to the blue-green Windows 7 screen. To restart the session, you must type in your password (and there's no point in using Lock if you haven't got one). This does not tie up the PC – there is a Switch User option which will allow someone else to use it.

- ■ Restart shuts down the PC completely, then starts it up again. You may need to do this after installing new software, or if the PC crashes (see page 46).

- ■ Sleep shuts down the screen and hard drive, but leaves the memory active. While suspended, the power consumption is very low, but the PC can be restarted almost instantly. This is a good alternative to a full shut down if you intend to restart in less than an hour or so.

- ■ With Hibernate, Windows makes a note of which programs are running, and which documents are open, then shuts down the PC. When you start it again, the programs and documents will be reopened automatically so that you can carry on from where you left off.

Windows essentials

2

Introduction

Windows 7 is an operating system – and more. An operating system handles the low-level interaction between the processor and the screen, memory, mouse, disk drives, printer and other peripherals. Windows 7 has drivers (control programs) for all PC-compatible processors and virtually all of the many PC peripherals on the market. The operating system is a bridge between the hardware of the computer and its applications – such as word processors and spreadsheets. As a result, whoever manufactured your PC and whatever type it is, as long as it can run the Windows 7 operating system, it can run any Windows 7 application. (It will also be able to run applications written for earlier versions of Windows.)

Although the operating system is the most important part of Windows, most of it is invisible. The visible part is the screen or Desktop. Windows is a graphical system. It uses icons (small images) to represent programs and files, and visual displays to show what is happening inside your PC. Many of the routine jobs are done by clicking on, dragging or otherwise manipulating these images, using the mouse or keyboard.

Windows is multi-tasking – it can run any number of programs at once. Each program runs in a separate area of the screen – a window – and these can be resized, moved, minimised or overlapped however you like. In practice, only a few will normally be active at the same time but that is more a reflection of the human inability to do several jobs simultaneously! A typical example of multi-tasking would be one program downloading material from the internet and another printing a long report, while you wrote a letter in a third.

This chapter covers the basic skills and concepts of working with Windows. You will learn how to use the mouse and the keyboard to select from menus, make choices, run programs and control the window layouts. You will also find out how to get help and how to cope when things go wrong.

Exploring the Desktop

Windows is a Graphical User Interface (or GUI, pronounced gooey). What this means is that you work mainly by using the mouse to point at and click on symbols on the screen, rather than by typing commands. It is largely intuitive – i.e. the obvious thing to do is probably the right thing – and it is tolerant of mistakes. Many can be corrected as long as you tackle them straight away, and many others can be corrected easily, even after time has passed.

One of the key ideas behind the design of Windows is that you should treat the screen as you would a desk, which is why Windows refers to the screen as the desktop. This is where you lay out your papers, books and tools, and you can arrange them to suit your own way of working. You may want to have more than one set of papers on the desktop at a time – so Windows lets you run several programs at once. You may want to have all your papers visible, for comparing or transferring data; you may want to concentrate on one, but have the others to hand. These – and other arrangements – are all possible.

Each program runs in its own window, and these can be arranged side by side, overlapping, or with the one you are working on filling the desktop and the others tucked out of the way, but still instantly accessible.

Just as there are many ways of arranging your desktop, so there are many ways of working with it – in fact, you are sometimes spoilt for choice!

It's your desktop. How you arrange it, and how you use it is up to you. This book will show you the simplest ways to use Windows 7 effectively.

- What you see on screen when you start Windows depends upon your Desktop settings and the shortcuts – the icons that you can click on to start programs – you are using.
- What the screen looks like once you are into your working session, is infinitely variable.
- Certain principles always apply and certain things are always there. It is the fact that all Windows applications share a common approach that makes Windows so easy to use.

2

Exploring the
Desktop (cont.)

Shortcuts   Desktop   Menu bar   Program windows   Gadgets

Start button   Quick Launch toolbar   Taskbar

Shortcuts – instant access to programs. You can create your own shortcuts.

Menu bar – gives access to a program's commands.

Ribbon – another way to access a program's commands.

Program windows – adjust their size and placing to suit yourself.

Desktop – you can change the background picture or pattern and its colours.

Start button – you should be able to start any program on your PC from its menu.

Taskbar – when a program is running it has a button here. Point to the button to see a thumbnail of the program's window (or windows, as there may be more than one). Click a thumbnail to bring that window to the front of the Desktop, or click the button to open a new window for that program. You can pin buttons to the Taskbar to give you quick access to programs – Internet Explorer and Media Player will be there already.

Gadgets – small programs, including a clock and various utilities that can draw information off the Internet.

Most Windows 7 operations can be handled quite happily by the mouse alone, leaving the keyboard for data entry. However, keys are necessary for some jobs, and if you prefer typing to mousing, it is possible to do most jobs from the keyboard. The relevant ones are shown here.

The function keys

Some operations can be run from these – for instance, F1 starts up the Help system in any Windows application.

The control sets

The Arrow keys can often be used instead of the mouse for moving the cursor. Above them are more movement keys, which will let you jump around in text. Insert and Delete are also here.

Key guide

Esc – to escape from trouble. Use it to cancel bad choices.

Tab – move between objects on screen.

Caps Lock – only put this on when you want to type a lot of capitals. The Caps Lock light shows if it is on.

Shift – use it for capitals and the symbols on the number keys.

Ctrl or Control – used with other keys to give keystroke alternatives to mouse commands.

🈯 – same as clicking the Start button on the screen.

Alt – used, like Ctrl, with other keys.

Backspace – rubs out the character to the left of the text cursor.

Enter – used at the end of a piece of text or to start an operation.

Delete – deletes files, folders and screen objects. Use with care.

Controlling the mouse

You can't do much in Windows until you have tamed the mouse. It is used for locating the cursor, for selecting from menus, highlighting, moving and changing the size of objects, and much more. It won't bite, but it will wriggle until you have shown it who is in charge.

The mouse and the cursor

There are two main types of mice.

One type has a ball beneath. Moving the mouse rolls the ball inside it. The ball turns the sensor rollers and these transmit the movement to the cursor. To control this type of mouse effectively you need a mouse mat or a thin pad of paper – it won't run well on a hard surface.

The other type uses infrared to scan the area beneath and work out which way the mouse has moved. This type needs some kind of image or pattern beneath it – it won't know where it is on a plain surface.

With either type:

- If you reach the edge of the mat or whatever you are using as a mouse run, so that you cannot move the cursor any further, pick up the mouse and plonk it back into the middle.
- You can set up the mouse so that when the mouse is moved faster, the cursor moves further. Watch out for this when working on other people's machines.

Mouse actions

- Point – move the cursor with your fingers off the buttons.
- Click – the left button to select a file, menu item or other object.
- Right-click (click the right button) to open a menu of commands that can be applied to the object beneath the pointer.

- Double-click to run programs. You can set the gap between clicks to suit yourself.
- Drag – keep the left button down while moving the mouse. Used for resizing, drawing and similar jobs.
- Drag and drop – drag an object and release the left button when it is in the right place. Used for moving objects.

Controlling the mouse (cont.)

2

See also

Controlling the mouse, page 227, to find out how to adjust the responsiveness of the mouse to suit your hand.

Using the Start menu

Clicking on the Start button at the bottom left of the screen opens the Start menu. Your menu will look a little different to mine – you can adapt the Start menu, and it will adapt to you automatically.

At the top left are links to your browser and email software (normally Internet Explorer and Live Mail).

Beneath these are links to your most-used programs – initially this will be empty.

At the bottom left is the All Programs link.

Just above the Start button is the Search box. Use this to track down files on your computer (see page 156).

At the top right are links to Documents, Pictures and other folders where documents and files are commonly stored.

You can configure your PC through the Control Panel (Chapter 9). You may have a link to the Printers, and/or a Connect To link which leads to your connections for going online.

Help and Support starts the Help system (page 42).

The arrow to the right of the Shut Down button offers alternative ways to end a session (see page 22).

Jargon buster

Document – Windows uses 'document' to mean any file created by any application. A word-processed report is obviously a document, but so is a picture file from a graphics package, a data file from a spreadsheet, a video clip, sound file – in fact, any file produced by any program.

Giving commands and making choices

Menus

In many Windows applications the commands and options are organised through menus. Menus drop down from the menu bar. To make one drop down, click on its name with the mouse, or press the Alt key and the underlined letter – usually the initial.

To select an item from a menu, click on it or type its underlined letter.

Some items are toggles. Selecting them turns an option on or off. ✔ beside the name shows that the option is on.

▶ after an item shows that another menu leads from it.

If you select an item with three dots ... after it, a dialogue box will open to get more information from you.

No menu – click to use the command

Point to open sub-menu

Toolbars

In some applications, including Explorer and Internet Explorer, a selection of the most commonly used commands is held on a toolbar. Some of the tools will lead directly to a command; others will open a menu. If there is a black down arrow to the right of a tool's name, it opens a menu.

Where there is a toolbar, the menu bar is normally hidden. To see it, press the Alt key.

Click to bring a tab to the front   Click the tool to apply the
                                           setting or run the command
Ribbon

Group   Click the arrow to see
                                           the tool's options

Click or press Alt +
the underlined letter

Keyboard shortcut

Opens a dialogue box

Giving commands and making choices (cont.)

Ribbons

In some applications, the commands and options are held on a Ribbon – the strip that runs across the top of the workspace. Ribbons often have several tabs, each with a different set of commands. Click on the tab name above the Ribbon to bring the tab to the front. Within each tab, the commands are held in groups.

To use a command, either click on its button, or click on its arrow to open a set of options.

Dialogue boxes

These vary, but will usually have these buttons:

OK – click when you have set the options, selected the file or whatever. This confirms your choices and closes the box.

Apply – click to fix the options selected so far, but keep the box open for further work.

Cancel – click if you decide the choices are all wrong.

 to get Help on items in the box.

Tabs and panels

Some dialogue boxes have several sets of options in them, each on a separate panel. These are identified by tabs at the top. Click on a tab to bring its panel to the front. Usually clicking OK on any panel will close the whole box. Use Apply when you have finished with one panel but want to explore others before closing.

Check boxes

These are used where there are several options, and you can use as many as you like at the same time.

✔ in the box shows that the option has been selected.

If the box is grey and the caption faint, the option is 'greyed out' – not available at that time for the selected item.

These are selected

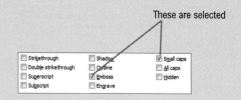

Radio buttons

These are used for either/or options. Only one of the set can be selected.

The selected option is shown by a black blob in the middle.

Rotation Type: Wobble

None
Spin
See-saw
Wobble
Tumble

Click here...

Select from the list

This one is selected

Surface Style

Solid Color

Texture

Reflection

Drop-down lists

If a slot has a down arrow button on its right, click the button to drop down a list.

Click on an item in the list to select.

Timesaver tip

Some commands have keyboard shortcuts. These are sometimes the Function keys, but often Ctrl + a letter. If there is a shortcut it will usually be shown on the menu after the command name.

2

Using context menus

If you click the right button on almost any object on screen in Windows 7, a short menu will open beside it. This contains a set of commands and options that can be applied to the object.

What is on the menu depends upon the type of object and its context – hence the name. Two are shown here to give an idea of the possibilities.

1 Files can be opened, sent to a removable disk or off in the mail, and deleted – amongst other things.

2 Adjust the clock and arrange the screen display.

The frame contains all the controls you need for adjusting the display.

1 The frame edge has a control system built into it. When a window is in Restore mode – i.e. smaller than full-screen – you can drag on the edge to make it larger or smaller.

2

2 The title bar is to remind you of where you are – in the active application (the one you are using) the Close button on the bar is red. Drag on the bar to move a window.

3 The Maximise, Minimise and Restore buttons change the display mode.

4 The Close button is one of several ways to close a window and the program that was running in it.

5 The Control menu can be used for changing the screen mode or closing the window.

6 Below the Title bar there will be either a Ribbon or a Menu bar, holding the program's commands and options.

7 The Scroll bars are present on the right side and bottom of the frame if the display contained by the window is too big to fit within it.

Important

Some applications can handle several documents at once, each in its own window. These are used in almost the same way as program windows. The applications usually have a Window menu containing controls for the document windows.

Scrolling in a window

What you can see in a window is often only part of the story. The working area of the application may well be much larger. If there are scroll bars on the side and/or bottom of the window, this tells you that there is more material outside the frame. The Sliders in the Scroll bars show you where your view is, relative to the overall display. Moving these allows you to view a different part of the display.

1. Drag the slider to scroll the view in the window. Drag straight along the bar or it won't work!

2. Click an arrow button to edge the slider towards it. Hold down for a slow continuous scroll.

3. Click on the bar beside the slider to make it jump towards where you are clicking.

Working area   Arrow buttons

Sliders

All programs are displayed on screen in windows, and these can normally have three modes:

- Maximised – filling the whole screen.
- Minimised – not displayed, though still present as a button on the Taskbar.
- Restore – adjustable in size and in position.

Clicking on the buttons in the top right corner of the frame is the simplest way to switch between Maximise and Restore modes, and to Minimise a window.

A window in Restore mode   A Maximised window   The current window is highlighted

Minimised – not visible except for this.

To make a window full-screen: Click 🔲.

To shrink a window to a Taskbar button: Click ▭. To redisplay it, click on its Taskbar button.

To restore a window to variable size: Click 🔲.

Timesaver tip

If you point to a Taskbar button, a thumbnail of its window will appear above it. If you have several windows of the same type open, e.g. two or three Word documents, there will be only one button, but it will have a thumbnail for each window. Click on the thumbnail to open the window.

 2

Did you know?

You can change window modes using the Control menu. Click the icon at the top left of the window to open it. This menu came from a variable-size window, so Restore is shown in grey as it does not apply. One from a full-screen window would have Maximise in grey.

You can open the menu using the keys:

Alt + Space opens the Control menu of an application.

Alt + – (minus) opens the Control menu of a document.

Arranging windows

If you want to have two or more windows visible at the same time, you will have to arrange them on your desktop. There are Windows tools that will do it for you, or you can do it yourself.

If you right-click the Taskbar, its menu has options to arrange the windows on the desktop. Similar options are on the Window menu of most applications, to set the layout within the programs.

Cascade places the windows overlapping with only the title bars of the back ones showing.

Show Windows Stacked and Show Windows Side by Side arrange open windows side by side, or one above the other – with more than three windows, the tiling is in both directions. As the window frames take up space, the actual working area is significantly reduced. Obviously, larger, high-resolution screens are better for multi-window work, but even on a 1280 × 1024 display you cannot do much serious typing in a tiled window.

1 Maximise or Restore the windows that you want to include in the layout. Minimise those that you will not be using actively.

2 Right-click the Taskbar to open its menu.

3 Select Show Windows Stacked or Show Windows Side by Side.

4 If you only want to work in one window at a time, Maximise it, and Restore it back into the arrangement when you have finished.

5 If you want to adjust the balance of the layout, you can move and resize the windows.

Important

Cascade works better than tiling on small screens.

Timesaver tip

It is generally simplest to work with the active window Maximised and any others Minimised out of the way.

When a window is in Restore mode – open but not full screen – it can be moved anywhere on the screen.

Moving windows

1 If the title bar isn't highlighted, click on the window to make it the active one.

2 Point at the title bar and hold the left button down.

3 Drag the window to its new position – you will only see a grey outline moving.

4 Release the button.

Important

If you are not careful it can be moved almost off the screen! Fortunately, at least a bit of the title bar will still be visible, and that is the handle you need to grab to pull it back into view.

Changing the window size

When a window is in Restore mode, you can change its size and shape by dragging the edges of the frame to new positions. Combined with the moving facility, this lets you arrange your desktop exactly the way you like it.

1 Move the pointer to the edge or corner that you want to pull in or out.

2 When you see the double-headed arrow, hold down the left mouse button and drag the outline to the required size.

3 Release the button.

Important

!

The resize pointers only appear when the pointer is just on an edge, and they disappear again if you go too far. Practise! You'll soon get the knack of catching them.

Timesaver tip

You can drag any edge or corner, but the quickest way to get a window the right size, in the right place, is to use the bottom right size handle to set the shape, then drag the window into position.

When you close a window, you close down the program that was running inside it.

If you haven't saved your work, most programs will point this out and give you a chance to save before closing.

There are at least five different ways of closing. Here are the simplest three:

- If the window is in Maximised or Restore mode, click the Close icon at the top right of the Title bar. (If your mouse control is not too good, you may well do this when you are trying to Maximise the window!)
- If the window has been Minimised onto the Taskbar, right-click on its button to open the Control menu and use Close.
- If you prefer working from keys, press Alt + F4.

Closing an active window

1 Click ⬚⬚ or press Alt + F4.

Closing from the Taskbar

2 Right-click the program's Taskbar button to get its menu.

3 Select Close.

4 If you have forgotten to save your work, take the opportunity that is offered to you.

Important

The right-click menu that pops up from a program's Taskbar button gives you a quick way to open any files that you have worked on recently with that program, or to start a new document in a new window. There is also an option to pin the program to the Taskbar. Use this with your favourite programs, so that they are always close to hand.

Getting Help and Support

Windows 7 has its own special Help and Support system. It's very comprehensive and has some excellent features, but – most unhelpfully – it looks and feels different from the standard application Help systems.

The main Windows 7 Help system is reached through the Help and Support item on the Start menu.

1 Click the Start button and select Help and Support.

2 Click a link to select a route into the Help system – choose Learn about Windows Basics this time.

Important

You can set up your system so that it only uses the Help on your hard disk, or get it to include the online Help and Support at Microsoft. If you have an always-on broadband connection to the Internet, online is normally the best choice, because it will give you access to more and better Help. To change the setting:

1 Click the Offline Help (or Online Help) button at the bottom right of the window.

2 Select Get online/offline Help to change the setting for the current session.

   or

3 Select Settings.

4 Tick (or clear) the Include Windows Online... option.

5 Click OK.

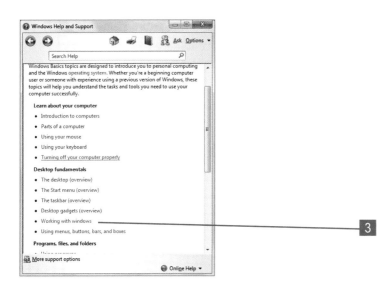

3 Scroll through the list and click on a topic.

4 Click on the terms in green to get an explanation of the terminology.

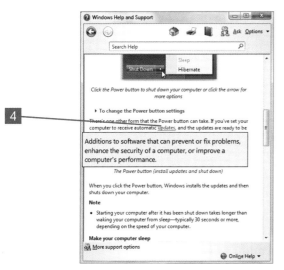

?

Did you know?

Text in blue is usually a link to another Help article. If the text has an arrow at the start, it tells you that clicking on it will start a program, open a dialogue box, or do something similar. The Help article will stay open, so that you can read it while you try out the program, or set options.

1. → Click to open Network and Sharing Center.
2. In the left pane, click **Set up a connection or network.**

Browsing Help topics

The Contents gives you access to the entire Help system. It is arranged into 15 main areas, which are subdivided into subtopics – each of which may be further subdivided.

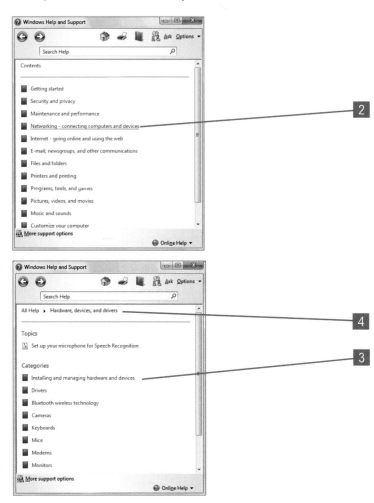

1 In the main Help and Support window, click the Browse Help topics link.

2 Folder headings have a block to the left. Click on a heading to open its folder. You will see a list of articles and headings for subtopics.

3 Article headings have a document icon on the left. Click on the heading to read the article.

4 At the top of the window you will see a list of the headings that you have clicked through to reach the current place. Click on any of these to jump back to that heading.

Timesaver tip

Don't forget the troubleshooting guides. You can reach these from the main Help and Support window. They can be very useful for solving common problems, such as difficulties with printers or other peripherals, or when you are trying to configure your Internet and email software. They will normally take you through a series of checks to diagnose problems and can often tell you what to do to cure them.

The Search box is present on every page of the Help system.

1 Type one or more keywords into the box and press the Enter key.

2 The 'best' 10 results, i.e. those which Windows 7 calculates as best matching your search, will be listed. Click on a heading to display the page.

3 If you don't find what you want, try different keywords. Sometimes it is better not to be too specific.

Jargon buster

Keyword – any word which might occur in the pages that you are looking for. If you give two or more, the system will only list pages which contain all those words.

2

Handling crashes with the Task Manager

Windows 7 is a pretty stable system, but things do go wrong. A 'crash' can occur at several levels.

- A program may simply misbehave – it will still run, but not respond or update the screen correctly. Close it – saving any open files – and run it again. If it still behaves badly, close down all your programs and restart the PC.

- The system will 'hang' – i.e. nothing is happening and it will not respond to the mouse or normal keyboard commands. If the Control + Alt + Del keystroke works, you can reach the Task Manager to close the offending application, which may get things moving again.

- You get a total lock up where it will not pick up Control + Alt + Del. Press the little restart button on the front of the PC. It is there for just these times!

Misbehaving program

1. Open the program's File menu and select Exit (or Close) – saving files if prompted.

2. Restart the program.

Hung system

3. Press Control + Alt + Delete together.

4. The desktop is replaced by a blue-green screen with options for locking or logging off. The last option is Start Task Manager. Click here.

5. At the Task Manager dialogue box, select the one marked 'not responding'.

6. Click End Task.

7. Restart the program.

Dead keyboard

8. Press the Restart button on the front of the PC.

The Internet

3

Introduction

This chapter aims to introduce some of the basic concepts of and ways of working on the Internet, and explores just a few of its almost infinite possibilities. I've tried to keep things as simple as possible, which hasn't been that difficult for me because the key Internet activities are essentially quite simple. There are all sorts of refinements and alternative ways of achieving similar results, and there are a few complexities, but these can be ignored until you are ready to deal with them. Of course, this simplified approach does mean that if things go wrong – and they do from time to time – you may not know how to deal with it. But let's be positive. As long as you follow the instructions, you should be fine, and an hour or so from now, you should have visited dozens of websites and found out all sorts of interesting things.

The software that is used here is Internet Explorer. This is supplied as part of Windows, and is a powerful piece of software – easy to use but with all the sophisticated features that you need to get the best out of browsing the World Wide Web. Only the main features are covered here, but that is all you need to get started. The screenshots are from Internet Explorer 8.0, the latest version at the time of writing.

To use this chapter, you need to have an Internet connection already in place, or if you haven't got one of your own yet, you need to visit one of the kids or a friend, or go to the public library – somewhere that you can get online.

Jargon buster

Browser – application specially designed for accessing and displaying the information in the World Wide Web. This is also true the other way: the web is an information system designed to be viewed on browsers.

Email – electronic mail, a system for sending messages and files across networks.

HTML – HyperText Markup Language, a system of instructions that browsers can interpret to display text and images. HTML allows hypertext links to be built into web pages.

Net – short for Internet. And Internet is short for interlinked networks, which is what it is.

Page – or web page, a document displayed on the web. It may be plain or formatted text; and may hold pictures, sounds and videos.

Web – World Wide Web. Also shortened to WWW or W3.

Discovering the Internet and the web

Let's start by clearing up a common misconception. The 'web' and the 'Internet' are not the same thing. Some people use the terms interchangeably, but they shouldn't.

- The **Internet** is the underlying framework. It consists of the computers, large and small, that store and process information for the Internet; the telephone wire, network cable, microwave links and other connections between them; and the software systems that allow them all to interact.

- The **World Wide Web** is the most visible and one of the simplest and most popular ways of using the net. It consists of – literally – billions of web pages, which can be viewed through browsers, such as Internet Explorer. The pages are constructed using HTML, that tells browsers how to display text and images, and how to manage links between pages. Clicking on a hypertext link in a page tells the browser to go to the linked page (or sometimes to a different type of linked file) – wherever it may be.

Email is another simple and very popular use of the Internet, and there are other more specialised Internet activities, as you will see later in this book.

3

Discovering Internet Explorer

There are several optional elements to the Internet Explorer window, so yours may well not look like this at the moment – but it could! Try and identify as many features as you can.

Start Internet Explorer by clicking the icon on the Taskbar, next to the Start button.

Start button

Internet Explorer icon

Title bar   Address bar   Tabs   Search bar

Command bar

Navigation buttons

Favourites bar

Explorer bar (displaying Favourites)

History tab

Divider

Status bar

Scroll bars

The toolbars

Title bar – shows the title of the web page, which is not the same as its URL.

Command bar – with tools for the most commonly-used commands. This and the Address and Links bars can be hidden if not wanted.

Address bar – shows the URL (Uniform Resource Locator, the address and filename) of the page. Addresses can be typed here.

Favourites bar – holds quick links to those places that you visit most often. There will be a few predefined links here to some of Microsoft's sites. You can remove any that you don't use and add your own.

Timesaver tip

The tools that you need regularly can all be found in the Toolbar. There is also a menu system, for those people who prefer to use the keyboard rather than the mouse. The menu bar is normally hidden – press Alt to make it visible.

Other features

Explorer bar – can be opened when it is needed to display your History (links to the places visited in the last few days) or your Favourites (links to selected pages), or to run a search for information. Clicking on a link in the Explorer bar will display its page in the main window.

Divider – click and drag on this to adjust the width of the Explorer bar. You may need more space when using the Explorer bar for a search.

Scroll bars – will appear on the right and at the bottom if a web page is too deep or too wide to fit into the window.

Status bar – shows the progress of incoming files for a page. When they have all downloaded, you'll see 'Done'. It also shows the address in a link when you point to it.

3

Discovering Internet Explorer (cont.)

The navigation tools

Use these to move between the pages you have already visited during the session:

1 Back takes you to the page you have just left.

2 Forward reverses the Back movement.

3 The drop-down page list allows you to select from the last dozen or so pages.

The standard toolbar

These buttons contain almost all of the controls that you need when you are online:

1 Home goes to your start page – your jumping off point into the web. This can be your own home page or any other.

2 Feeds are used to alert you to new content in web pages. Not all sites offer a feeds service – click the button when you are on a page to see if feeds are available from it.

3 Email – starts your email application and checks for new messages.

4 Print prints the current page (text and graphics).

5 Page opens a menu. Its commands are related to the content of pages. Note these useful ones:

- Copy copies text or images for pasting into a document.
- Save As stores a copy of the page.
- Send Page/Link by Email connects you to Live Mail to send someone the page, or a link to it.
- Zoom enlarges the text and graphics.
- Text size enlarges, or reduces, the text size.

6 Safety opens a menu of commands relating to safety and privacy online. Note these:

- Delete Browsing History – opens a dialogue box where you can delete the temporary files and records of sites you have visited. Do this to save disk space and/or to wipe out your tracks.
- InPrivate Browsing – opens a new window where you can browse without leaving tracks. (See page 67)
- SmartScreen Filter – helps to protect your PC against malicious websites. This should be turned on.

7 Tools also leads to a menu. Its commands are more varied – key ones include:

- Pop-up Blocker: turn this on to block pop-up windows – usually carrying adverts – opening when you visit web pages.
- Full screen removes the toolbars and uses the entire screen to display a page.

▶

- The Toolbars submenu controls the display of toolbars and sidebars.
- Internet Options allow you to configure Explorer to suit your needs.

8 Help opens a menu offering alternative ways to get help.

Delete Browsing History

InPrivate Browsing

SmartScreen Filter

Pop-up Blocker

Full Screen

Toolbars

Internet Options

See also

See Using Favourites on page 60 and Viewing the History list on page 64 for more on these uses of the Explorer bar.

See Printing web pages on page 69 to find out about the Print options.

Timesaver tip

If you are having trouble downloading a web page, it may help to start again from scratch. Click Stop, then Refresh.

Browsing the web

If you want to 'browse' the web, all you need is a good place to start, and one of the best places is a net directory – a site with sets of organised links to other sites. And one of the best directories is the one at Google. What makes it so useful is that it is extremely comprehensive, but all the sites listed there have been recommended by someone at some point. Quality control is rare on the web.

 1 Go to Google by typing this address into the Address bar: www.google.co.uk

2 In the links across the top of the page, click 'more' to drop down a list, then click the last entry, 'even more'.

3 Click on the Directory link.

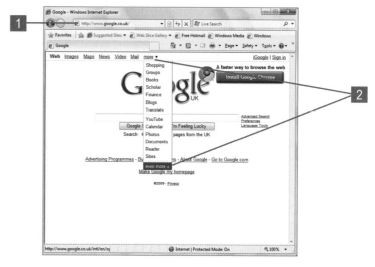

Timesaver tip

If you know what you are looking for, it is quicker to search for it – see page 58.

4 In the Web directory, click on the heading or subheading of a topic that interests you. Note that in each category, only the first three or four subheadings are visible at this point – select the main heading to see the full set.

Important

A hyperlink (link for short) is a connection to another web page. When you click on a link, Internet Explorer goes to that page and displays it. You know when you are on a link because the arrow pointer becomes a hand.

Browsing the web (cont.)

When you are looking for material at Google don't worry too much if you are not sure which category your topic will fit into. The directory is so well cross-referenced that any reasonable start point should get you there.

The directory is organised as a hierarchy with many levels. At each level there are three sets of links:

- At the top are links to Categories – most of these are subdivisions of the current category.

- The second set are Related Categories – places elsewhere in the hierarchy.

- The third set are the Site listings.

As you work down through the levels, the first set shrinks, and the third set grows.

5 Use the category links to get down through two or three levels to reach a specialised topic of your choice.

6 Scroll down the page to see the links to sites.

7 Read the listings, and click on one to go to its site.

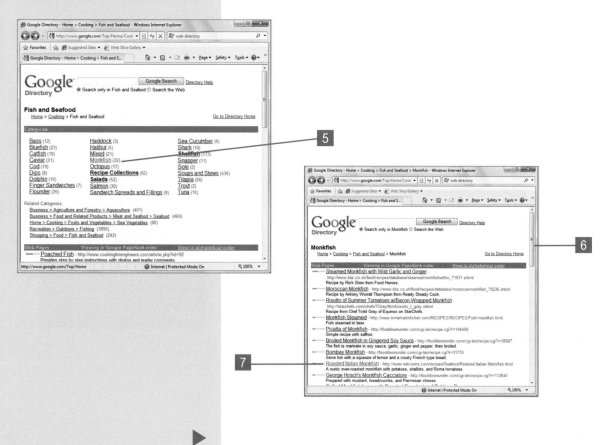

There's so much to see on the web! In fact, there's too much. You can often find links to scores – or even hundreds – of sites on a topic, so you have to learn to be selective or you can waste an awful lot of time online. Dip into a site to get an idea of what it is like, and if it's not really what you are looking for, move on and try elsewhere.

8 When the new page has loaded in, read to see if it is of interest. If you see a link that looks promising, click on it to find out where it leads.

9 If you want to go back to the previous page at the site, or back from there to Google, click the Back button.

10 If you want to start browsing a new topic, either work your way back to the top level page in the Google directory, or start again by typing www.google.co.uk into the Address bar.

3

! Important

Sometimes when you click on a link, the new page opens in a new window. This can be useful as it means that the previous page is still there in the original Internet Explorer window. However, there are a couple of catches. It can get a bit confusing if you have too many windows open at once, and the Back button only works within the same window. As a general rule, if a site has opened in a new window, close the window when you have finished with that site.

Searching the web

Search the web

1 Go to Google at:
www.google.co.uk

2 Type in one or more words to
describe what you would like
to find, e.g. 'bayeux tapestry',
or 'bridge club bradford'.

3 If you are looking for an
organisation or supplier in the
UK, or you want information
about something UK-based,
select the pages from the UK
option.

4 Press the Enter key or click
the Google Search button.

5 The results show the names
and the first couple of lines of
details from the matching
pages. Scroll through to find
the ones that look most
promising.

6 Click on the page name link to
go to the page.

7 Use ⬅ to return to Google
if you want to follow up
other links.

Web directories offer one approach to finding material on the
web. Search engines offer another, and this is often the best
way if you are looking for very specific information. A search
engine is a site that has compiled an index to web pages, and
which lets you search through the index. There are several
dozen search engines, and they compile their indices in
different ways and to different levels of completeness, but
some of the best know what's on 80% or more of the pages on
the web. The most complete and the most effective is Google.
It is so well used and loved that searching the web is now
often called 'googling'.

You search by giving one or more words to specify what you are
looking for. Try to be specific. If you search for 'football', 'bridge'
or 'gardening' you will get millions of links to possible pages.

Google has links to over 8 billion pages in its index! Which is why you have to be as specific as possible when looking for particular information. However, sometimes it pays to be less specific, as this can produce leads that you might never have thought of yourself.

It doesn't matter too much if you get millions of results from a search as the good stuff tends to be listed at the top. (Google has developed some very clever systems for rating pages.)

3

Important

You will find a link to the next page at the bottom of the results listing, but as a general rule, if you don't see anything useful in the first page, subsequent pages are unlikely to be any better. Try a new search instead, with different words.

Using Favourites

A favourite is an address stored in an easily-managed list. To return to a favourite place, you simply click on it in the list.

Favourites are accessed through the Favourites Centre, in the Explorer bar on the left of the screen. The bar will normally close automatically after you have selected a Favourite. If you want to keep it open – so that you can visit several places – click the pin to fix it in place.

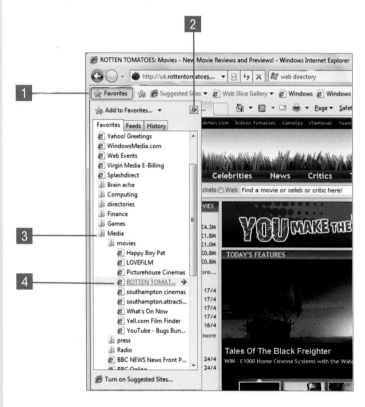

1 Click the Favourites button to open the Favourites Centre.

2 If you want to keep the bar open, click the Pin icon in the top right.

3 If the Favourites is in a folder, click on the name to open the folder. Repeat if necessary to open a sub-folder.

4 Click on a Favourite to link to its website.

Did you know? **?**

Even if you haven't yet added a Favourite of your own, there should be some already in the list – mainly to Microsoft's sites.

Internet addresses are a pain to type. One mistake and either you don't get there at all, or you find yourself at a totally unexpected site. (Try www.microsfot.com sometime.) Favourites are one way of being able to return to a site without having to retype its address.

Adding a Favourite

1. Find a good site!

2. Open the Favourites Centre, and click Add to Favourites.

3. The Add a Favourite dialogue box will open. Internet Explorer will have derived the Name from the page. If you are happy with the name and want to add the link to the main Favourites list, click Add.

   otherwise

4. Edit the suggested name, or type a new one – you want something that will work well as a menu item, so aim for short but meaningful.

5. To store it in a folder, click the Create in button to expand the folder list.

6. If there is a suitable folder, click on it.

7. If not, click New Folder.

8. Type a name for the folder and click Create in.

9. Back at the Add a Favourite dialogue box, click Add.

Organising your Favourites

You can store your favourites in one simple list, but this soon gets unwieldy. If there are more than about twenty items, the menu takes up too much screen space and it can be hard to find the favourite you want. The solution is to organise your favourites into folders, which then become sub-menus in the Favourites system. It's easy to create new folders and to move entries into them.

1 Open the Favourites Centre, click the arrow to the right of Add to Favourites and select Organise Favourites from the menu.

2 Click New Folder.

3 A new folder will appear. Give it a suitable name.

4 Drag the link on to the folder and drop it in. If you pause over the folder first, it will open and you can then place the link exactly where you want it in the list.

or

5 Select the link and click Move.

6 Select the folder from the list.

7 Click OK.

As you browse, each page is recorded in the History list as an Internet shortcut – i.e. a link to the page. Clicking the History button opens the History list in the Explorer bar. Click a link from here to go to the page.

If you are online at the time, Internet Explorer will connect to the page. If you are offline, it will display the page if all the necessary files are still available in the temporary Internet files folder, otherwise it will ask you to connect.

1 Click on the Favourites button.

2 Click on the History tab in the favourites toolbar.

3 Click on the name to open the day and the site folders (if relevant in that view).

4 The Favourites pane will normally close after you have selected a link. If you want to keep it open, click the Pin button.

5 To close a folder, click on its name.

6 Click ⊠ to close the Explorer bar when you have finished.

3

Viewing the History list

The History list can be viewed in four ways:

- By Date groups the links into folders by date and then by site. This is useful if you know when you were last there, but not the name of the site – and you may well not know where a page was if you reached it through a hyperlink.
- By Site groups the links into folders by site. This is probably the most convenient view most of the time.
- By Most Visited lists individual page links in the order that you visit them most. If there are search engines or directories that you regularly use as start points for browsing sessions, they will be up at the top of the list.
- By Order Visited Today lists the individual pages in simple time order. Use this view to backtrack past the links that are stored in the drop-down list of the Back button.

1 In the Explorer bar, click the drop-down bar at the top of the list to see the View options.

2 Select the view which you think will enable you to find the required page fastest.

Timesaver tip

If the History list starts to get clogged up, you can delete sites or individual pages within sites. Right-click on the site or page and select Delete from the pop-up menu that appears.

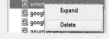

When you visit a web page, the files that create it are downloaded onto your PC. These files are retained, and if you return to that page, either during the same session or later, it will then use the stored files, which is quicker than downloading them again. It also means that you can revisit pages offline.

You can set the amount of storage space to suit the way you surf and the size of your hard disk. If you have plenty of space and you tend to go back to sites a lot – perhaps following up a succession of links from one start point, or perhaps because you like to revisit sites offline – give yourself a big cache. If space is a problem, cut the cache right down. And if you need to free up the disk space, delete all the stored files.

You can also choose when Internet Explorer should check for newer versions of the stored pages. The 'Automatically' setting should do the job – this will check at the first visit in a session, but select the 'Every visit to the page' option if your favourite sites are fast-changing ones, e.g. news sites.

Managing temporary Internet files

1 Use Tools, Internet Options… to open the dialogue box.

2 If you need to clear space on your disk quickly, click Delete.

3 In the Browsing History area, click Settings.

4 Choose when to check for newer versions of stored pages.

5 Use the arrow buttons, or edit the numbers to set the amount of disk space.

6 Click OK.

3

Controlling the History

If you visit a lot of sites during your online sessions, and/or have set the number of days to keep the History links to a high value, then your History list could get very long. Beyond a certain point, its value as an aid to better browsing starts to diminish. You are probably best to set the days to no more than seven. The situations in which the History is most useful are those where you want to look back in leisurely offline time at pages that you glanced at while online, and you are most likely to do that either on the same day or within a couple of days. When you find sites that you will want to return to regularly, don't use the History – add them to your Favourites.

1 Use Tools, Internet Options… to open the Internet Options dialogue box.

2 Click Settings in the Browsing History area.

3 Type a new value or use the arrows to adjust the number of days.

4 Click OK to save the change and exit.

Important

The Delete button will open a dialogue box where you can delete the History list, and/or the temporary files and cookies that will have been stored on your PC as you have been browsing. Do this to save disk space and/or to wipe out your tracks. See also InPrivate Browsing on the next page.

The History list is very useful for popping back to places for a second look, but if other people have access to the PC, they can tell where you have been by looking at the History. If you prefer to keep some of your browsing private, then rather than go back and delete items from the History list (see page 64) or clear the whole list (see page 66), you can use the InPrivate Browsing facility.

Browsing in private

1. Click Safety on the Command bar to open the menu.

2. Select InPrivate Browsing.

3. A new window will open. You will see 'InPrivate' to the left of the Address bar. Wherever you go now, there will be no trace left in your History list or in the stored addresses in the Address bar.

4. When you have finished your private browsing, close the window. The normal – un-private – window should still be there.

Timesaver tip

You can turn on InPrivate Browsing with the keyboard shortcut – Ctrl + Shift + P.

Previewing before you print

A sheet of A4 paper and a computer screen are rather different shapes, and pages can be laid out on the screen in different ways. What this means is that you can never be entirely sure what a web page will look like when it is printed, or how many sheets it will be printed on – unless you use Print Preview. If the preview is acceptable, you can send it straight to the printer; if adjusting the layout might give a better printout, you can open the Page Setup dialogue box and change the settings.

Using Print Preview

1 Click the arrow by the Print tool to drop down the menu and select Print Preview.

2 Use the arrows to work through the pages.

3 Change the Zoom level to look at details or the overall layout.

4 If you want to adjust the page layout, click the Page Setup button (see the next page for more on this).

5 To print the page(s), click 🖶.

6 To return to the normal web page display without printing, click ✖.

If you just want a printed copy of the whole of the current page, you simply click the Print button. Sometimes you need to control the printout – you may only want part of a long page or a section of a framed page, or you may want to print sideways on the paper (landscape orientation), or print several copies. In these cases, you need to go into the Print dialogue box.

Timesaver tip

You can sometimes get better results by copying part or all of a page into your word processor and printing it from there.

Important

The Print and Print Preview commands are also on the menu that drops down from the Print button.

3

Printing web pages

1 To print the current page, just as it is, click .

2 If you only want to print part of a page, use the mouse to select it now – you may sometimes find that additional items get selected alongside the part that you wanted. That's just the way web pages are!

3 If the screen page is very long, click the Print drop-down arrow and select Print Preview, to see which pages you want to print on paper.

4 Click the Print drop-down arrow and select Print.

5 Select the pages, if relevant.

6 Set the number of copies.

7 Click on Print.

Installing add-ons

Browsers can display only formatted text and GIF and JPG graphics; but add-ons extend the range of files that they can handle. These are extensions to the browser, not independent applications. Some are present from the start, others can be downloaded from Microsoft or other sources when they are needed. Whenever you meet a file that needs an add-on, it will normally be accompanied by a link that you can use to get the software. Exactly what you have to do to download and install the add-on varies, though the process is almost always straightforward and there are usually clear instructions. Here, for example, is what happens when you install RealPlayer.

1 You will be alerted when you need an add-on, and you will be offered a link to a site from whence you can download it. Follow the link.

2 At the site, read the instructions. If there are different versions of the software, choose the one for your computer system.

3 Start the download. You will be asked if you want to run the software. Click Run.

4 Wait while the file downloads. RealPlayer is small, so it won't take long, but some applications run to several megabytes and may take a while to download.

Important

With some add-ons you install them by saving a file, then running that installation file from Windows. Others, like Real, perform the installation automatically. In all cases, follow the prompts, and use your common sense.

70

5   As you selected Run at step 3, the installation will start automatically once the download is complete.

6   The User Account Control routine will check with you that you really want to install the software – this is your protection against viruses sneaking in and installing themselves without you knowing.

7   Set the options as required. You can make RealPlayer the default instead of Media Player, if you like – it's a matter of preference.

?

Did you know?

Add-ons are almost always free. Their manufacturers make money by charging for the applications that create the files that the add-ons play.

3

Getting Adobe Reader

Adobe Reader is one add-on that you really should have, as it is what you need to view and print PDF documents. People use PDFs for booklets and brochures, for books (this one went to the printer's as a PDF) and for paper sculpture kits (see the Did you know?) – in fact, for any document where well-formatted text and images are needed. PDF stands for Portable Document Format, and it is portable. A PDF file can be viewed on any computer or printed on any printer and the result will be the same.

1 When you try to open or download a PDF file you should find a link to get the Adobe Reader 'Plug-in'. Click it.

or

2 Head directly to Adobe at www.adobe.com and follow the links to get the Reader.

3 Follow the instructions to Download and install the Reader.

4 When you next come across a PDF file, Reader will start up inside Internet Explorer. Use its toolbar buttons to save, print or do other work with the document.

Did you know?

Yamaha Motor Company have some lovely paper model kits (in PDFs) for free downloading – great for the grandkids on rainy afternoons! Find them at www.yamaha-motor.co.jp. Search for 'papercraft' and follow the links.

Microsoft offers a set of programs – Windows Live Essentials – for free download. I would not call them all 'essential', but some are certainly useful. All of them, to a greater or lesser extent, make use of the Internet for sharing and exchanging text, images or other files with other people.

The programs are:

- Messenger – for real-time exchange of messages and images with other Messenger users

- Mail – a fully equipped email program. You will need this and we will be looking at it in Chapter 4.

- Writer – for creating and uploading text and images to blogging sites.

1 Click the Start button.

2 Click the arrow to the right of Getting Started, and on its submenu select Get Windows Live Essentials.

3 When you get to the Windows Live site, click the Download button.

4 At the File Download dialogue box, click Run. What you are getting at this point is just a control program, which is quite small.

5 When the file is downloaded it will start to run automatically, and the User Account Control dialogue box will check that you mean to run this. You do!

6 The main download is over 130Mb and will take a few minutes. Once it comes in, the Live software will begin to install.

Downloading Windows Live (cont.)

7 You will be shown a service agreement – accept it.

8 Select the programs that you want to install.

9 Click Install, and go and have a cuppa – installation takes a while, and there's nothing more for you to do.

10 When the installation has finished, you will find a new folder on your Start menu – click All Programs, then click Windows Live to start exploring your new programs.

- Photo Gallery – for organising, editing, printing and otherwise working with your digital photos. This is very useful, as you will see in Chapter 8.

- Movie Maker – for editing and publishing home videos.

- Family Safety – filters and other controls to restrict how children can use the PC and what they can access on the Internet.

- Toolbar – an add-on to Internet Explorer giving quick links to the Windows Live facilities.

Some of you may have been working on someone else's connection while reading this chapter, so before we leave, let's have a look at how to get connected. It's not hard. When I first went online, in the late 1980s, getting connected required relatively expensive equipment and quite a lot of technical know-how – and there wasn't that much to do once you got online! Today, the costs are minimal, no technical knowledge is needed, and the online possibilities are amazing.

To get connected you need four things:

- A computer – any reasonably modern computer will do. It does not need to be state-of-the-art or top-of-the-range. If you are buying a new system, the cheapest Windows 7 PC will do the job, or even a second-hand Windows XP or Vista machine – as long as it is in good condition. Apple Macs are fine, and less susceptible to viruses (which are mainly written by Windows programmers), but they are more expensive to buy and there is less software available for Apples. Cost: under £400 for a desktop PC complete with Windows, Internet Explorer, a word processor, and other entry-level but adequate software. Spend more only if you need a higher specification machine, or more sophisticated software for other uses.
- A modem – the device which links the computer to the phone line. You need a different type of modem for a dial-up connection down a normal phone line than for a broadband connection. Modern PCs are usually sold with a standard modem built-in, and so are ready for a dial-up connection. If you take the broadband alternative, a suitable modem will be supplied as part of the deal.
- A phone line – or more to the point, a phone socket within reach of the computer. If necessary, you can get extension phone leads at any good DIY store. Cost: £5–£10.
- An account with an Internet service provider – the company that will link you to the Internet and provide you with your email address and web space if you want to set up a site.

How do I choose an ISP?

There are basically three types of ISP account.

- A broadband connection gives high-speed access to the internet. This uses the normal phone line, but the line has to be reconfigured at the exchange before it can be used. Not all local exchanges have this capacity, so the first thing to do is to check that broadband is available in your area. Broadband users can connect at the start of the day and leave it connected until they shut down – it costs nothing and causes no problems as the phone can be used for normal calls while the computer is online.

There are several variables: speed, download limits, number of email addresses that you can run from one account, and whether or not you are given web space. The cost will vary to match, from around £15 to £30 a month. You only need the very high speeds and high

Getting
connected (cont.)

download limits if you intend to download a lot of music or videos. All broadband ISPs offer a free modem, but you must sign up for a minimum of 1 year.

Broadband providers include AOL, Orange, BTInternet, Virgin and most other phone companies.

- A monthly contract dial-up account. This will work on any phone line – you can even connect through a mobile if you have a suitable lead. Though far slower than broadband, dial-up is what we all managed with perfectly happily until recently. Expect to pay £15 a month, and to get unlimited access on an 0800 line.
- A pay-as-you-go dial-up account. These also run on the standard phone line. They typically cost 1p per minute, with the charging done through your phone bill as the connections are

to 0844 or 0845 numbers. If you mainly use the Internet for email, with occasional dips into the web to look things up, then pay-as-you-go can be an economic solution – one brief phone call a day to collect and receive your email should add up to a little over £1 a month. Dial-up account providers include AOL, Orange and many smaller firms, including my own excellent TCP.

Important

The problem is, you don't really know what you need until you have been active online for a while. So here's a suggestion. Several ISPs – notably AOL – offer a free month's trial of their dial-up service. Try it. See how you get on, and make an informed decision at the end of the month.

Email

4

Introduction

The World Wide Web may well be the most glamorous aspect of the Internet and the one that grabs newcomers, but email is the aspect that many people find the most useful in the long run. It is quick, reliable and simple to use.

- Email is quick. When you send a message to someone, it will normally reach their mailbox within minutes – and usually within half an hour. However, it will only be read when the recipient collects the mail, and that may be anything from a few minutes later to when they get back from holiday.
- Email is reliable. As long as you have the address right, the message is almost certain to get through. And on those rare occasions when it doesn't, you will usually get it back with an 'undeliverable' note attached.
- Email is simple to use. You can learn the essential skills in minutes – as you will see very shortly!

What you'll do

Understand email

Start Live Mail

Explore the commands

Read an email message

Add an address to Windows Contacts

Find a contact

Write a message

Reply to an email

Forward a message

Attach a file to a message

Insert a photo into a message

Save an attached file

Open an attachment

Adjust the layout

Control the Reading pane

Understanding email

It may help you to have an overview of the technology behind email, so you can use it more efficiently and are less likely to get fazed when things don't quite go according to plan!

When you send an email message, it does not go direct to your recipient, as a phone call does. Instead it will travel through perhaps a dozen or more computers before arriving at its destination – in the same way that snail mail passes through several post offices and depots. The message goes first to the mail server at your ISP. This will work out which computer to send it to, to help it towards its destination. The server will normally hold the message briefly, while it assembles a handful of messages to send to the next place – in the same way that the Post Office sorts and bags its mail. Each mail server along the way will do the same thing, bundling the message with others heading in the same direction. This method gives more efficient Internet traffic and at the cost of very little delay – most messages will normally be delivered in less than an hour.

However, your recipients won't necessarily be reading the message within the hour. The delivery is to their mail boxes at their service providers. People only get their email when they go online to collect it. (Though with a broadband account and automated collection it can feel as if its delivered.)

Email messages are sent as text files. A plain text message will normally be very short, as it takes only one byte to represent a character (plus about 10% more for error-checking). A ten-line message, for example, will make a file of around 1 Kb, and that can be transmitted in about 3 seconds. Images, video clips and other files can be sent by mail (see page 89) but they must first be converted into text format. You don't need to worry about how this is done, as Windows Mail will do all the conversion automatically. What you do need to know is that conversion increases the size of files by around 50%, so even quite small images can significantly increase the time it takes to send or receive messages.

Jargon buster

Error-checking – the techniques used to make sure that data sent over the Internet arrives intact. If a block of data is damaged, it is sent again.

Jargon buster

ISP (Internet service provider) – the company that supplies your connection to the Internet.

Jargon buster

Mail server – computer that stores and handles email.

Jargon buster

Plain text – text without any layout or font formatting

Live Mail is the email software supplied with Windows 7. It is very simple to use – you can pick up your mail with one click of a button, and though it takes a little more to send a message, there's nothing complicated in it.

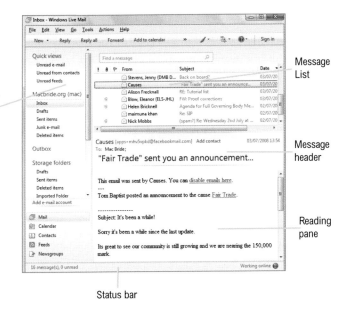

Folder pane

Message List

Message header

Reading pane

Status bar

1 Start Live Mail from the Start menu.

2 Identify the marked areas. If you are working on a friend's PC, check before you read any messages! If it's your own PC, and the software has been installed recently, you should have a welcome message from Microsoft.

Jargon buster

Snail mail – post hand-delivered by the postman.

4

▶

Email 79

Starting Live Mail (cont.)

The three key elements of the Live Mail window are the Folders pane, Message List and the Reading pane. There are another six elements that can be included in the display. Apart from the Message List, every element is optional and can be easily switched off if you decide that you do not want it.

- The Message List is the only part of the display which is not optional, but even here you can control the layout and which items are displayed.

- The Folder pane shows your email and news folders. New email folders can be created if needed, and newsgroup folders are created automatically when you subscribe to groups. The contents of the current folder are displayed in the Message List.

- The Reading pane displays the current message from the Message List. If this pane is turned off, messages are displayed in a new window. The pane can sit below or beside the List – below is usually more convenient.

- The Message header repeats the From and Subject details from the Message List.

- The Status bar, as always, helps to keep you informed of what's going on. Amongst other things, it tells you how many messages are in a folder, and shows the addresses behind hyperlinks in emails.

New Reply to All Add to Calendar Junk Colour Help

Reply Forward Delete Sync Options

Live Mail has a lot of commands that most of us will rarely use, and if you don't join the newsgroups, there are some that you will never use at all. In practice, the commands that you will use regularly can be found on buttons on the toolbar.

New

Click this button to start a new message in plain text or with the default formatting, or click the arrow to open a drop-down list.

Reply

Starts a new message to the sender of the current message.

Reply all

Sends a reply to all the people who had copies of the message.

Forward

Copies the message into the New Message window, ready for you to send it on to another person.

Delete

Deletion is a two-stage process. Clicking this button transfers the selected message(s) to the Deleted Items folder. Messages are then deleted from there when you close Live Mail or when you delete them from the Deleted Items folder.

Sync

Checks the mailbox(es) at your mail provider to see if there are any new messages, and sends any currently sitting in the Outbox. The options that drop down from this allow you to check only your main mail account, or all of them, or mail, feeds and newsgroups all at once.

> **Important**
>
> Live Mail can handle feeds and newsgroups as well as email, but there is not room in this book to cover them.

4

Reading an email message

Unlike snail mail, email does not get delivered directly to you. Instead, it goes into a mailbox at the provider and you must go online to get it. You can set Live Mail to check for new mail automatically on start-up and/or at regular intervals while you are online, or you can pick up your mail when you feel like it.

When messages arrive, they are dropped into the Inbox folder. Opening them for reading is very straightforward. After reading, you can reply if you like, and the message can be deleted or you can move them to another folder – you might want to keep some for future reference. You can also just leave the message in the Inbox for the time being.

1 Start Live Mail.

2 If you are not online already, get connected now.

3 Live Mail will normally check for new messages when it first starts. If it hasn't, or you want to check again now, click the Sync button, or open the Tools menu and select Sync, then wait while the messages come in.

4 Select Inbox in the Folder pane, if necessary.

5 Click anywhere in the header line in the Message List to open the message in the Reading pane. After reading the message…

6 If you don't want it any more, right-click on it and select Delete.

7 If you want to leave it in the Inbox for the time being, click on the header line of the next message to read that.

8 If you want to respond to it, click Reply.

Windows Contacts isn't just a convenience, it is also an essential tool for email. Addresses are rarely easy to remember and if you get just one letter wrong, the message won't get through. But if an address is stored in your Contacts, you can pick it from there whenever you need it.

Addresses can be added to the Contacts in two ways: you can type them in directly, or if you are replying to people who have written to you, you can get Live Mail to copy their addresses into the Contacts.

Adding an address to Windows Contacts

1. Open the Go menu and select Contacts.

2. When the Contacts window opens, click the New button's arrow and select Contact.

3. The dialogue box has tabs for different sets of contact details, but most of the time you can put all you need in using the Quick add tab. This should be at the front – select it if it is not.

4. Type in the person's first and last names and the email address. Add the phone and company details if you like.

5. Click Add contact.

4

Finding a contact

If there are only a couple of dozen entries in your Contacts, you should be able to find a person simply by scrolling through the list. As the numbers rise, it can take longer to spot the entry that you need. Searching is the answer.

If you type a few letters of the name into the Search box, Contacts will filter the list to display only the names that match. The more of the name that you type, the more the displayed set will shrink.

1 If Contacts is not active, open the Go menu and select Contacts.

2 Type the first few letters – or any part of the name – into the Search box at the top right of the window.

3 Check the display as it is filtered, to see if the entry has been found.

4 Type more of the name if necessary.

5 When you find the person you want, right-click on the name.

6 Select Edit Contact to open the properties dialogue box where you can change or add more details.

7 Select Send email to start writing a message.

8 Select Delete contact if it is no longer needed.

Timesaver tip

Sometimes, email addresses will go into the Contacts list without their matching real names. If the email address bears no resemblance to their real name – and it happens – then the search will be more difficult. Try to remember something of the address, or of the company that the person works for, and search on that.

Messages are written in the New Message window. The main part of this is the writing area, but in the top part of the window there are several boxes which must be attended to.

- To: is the address of the recipient(s).
- Cc: (carbon copy) is for the addresses of those people, if any, to whom you want to send copies.
- You can also have Bcc: (blind carbon copy) recipients if you select their names from the Select Recipients dialogue box. These people will not be listed, as the To and Cc recipients will be, at the top of the message.
- Subject: a few words outlining the nature of your message, so that your recipients know what's coming.

Writing a message

1. Open the File menu, point to New and select Mail Message or click the New button.

2. Click the To button, to the left of the top slot to open the Select contacts dialogue box.

3. Select a contact and click the To:->, Cc:-> or Bcc:-> buttons, to copy the name into the recipient box.

   Repeat Step 3 if you want to add more recipients.

4. Click OK to return to the New Message window.

5. Enter a Subject for the message.

6. Type the message.

4

Email 85

Writing a message (cont.)

A message can be sent immediately after it has been written, or stored in the Outbox to be sent later. If you have a broadband connection, you would normally be online while you are writing the messages, and would send messages immediately. If you connect through the normal phone line, being online ties up the phone and (probably) costs money. In this case, you would be better to write your messages offline, store them in the Outbox then send all the new ones in one batch.

You can set the options so that either the Send button will send immediately or it will store messages. If you want to handle a message differently, there are Send and Send Later commands.

7 Click Send to use the default Send option.

or

8 Open the File menu and select Send Message or Send Later.

9 When you have finished all your writing, if there are messages in the Outbox, click the Sync button, or open the Tools menu and select Sync. If you aren't online, the Connect dialogue box will appear, ready to connect to your ISP.

Timesaver tip

If you forget to send the messages in the Outbox, Live Mail will prompt you to send them before closing down. And if you close down without sending them, it will prompt you again the next time that you start Live Mail.

Replying to someone else's email is the simplest and most reliable way to send a message, because the address is already there for you.

When you start to reply, the original text may be copied into your message. You can decide whether or not this should happen, and how the copied text is to be displayed – these are controlled from the Tools, Options dialogue box. For the moment, go with the default settings.

1. When you click the Reply tool the Compose window will open.

2. The To: field will already have the email address in it – though it may actually display the person's name. Don't worry about that.

3. The Subject: field will have the original Subject text, preceded by 'Re:'. Edit this if you like.

4. The message area may have the original text copied in. You can edit or delete this if you like.

5. Add you own message.

6. Click Send.

4

Forwarding a message

If someone sends you a message that you would like to share with other people, you can do this easily by forwarding. The subject and message are copied into the New Message window, so all you have to do is add the address of the recipients and any comments of your own.

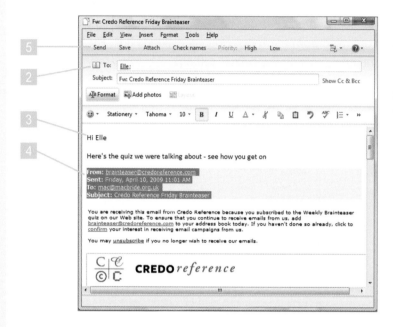

1. Select the message and click Forward.

2. Add the To: address.

3. Add any comments of your own.

4. Trim out any unwanted material from the original.

5. Click Send.

Images, documents, music, programs and other non-text files can be sent by email, attached to messages. As the mail system was designed for transmitting plain text, other files have to be converted to text for transfer, and back to binary on receipt. Live Mail handles these conversions for you, but you need to be aware of the conversion, because it increases the size of files by about 50%. Big files get even bigger.

Important

If you have a dial-up connection, very large attached files can be a problem. If the connection is broken during transmission, you have to start sending or receiving again from scratch, and messages are sent in the order in which they are created or arrive in your mailbox – so a big file will block your communications until it gets through. And remember that this also applies to the people to whom you are sending messages – don't send people big files unless they want them!

Inserting a photo into a message

Photos can be sent as attachments, but they can also be inserted into the body of the message, just as images can be inserted into a Word or WordPad document.

1. Start a new message as usual.

2. Click the Photos button beneath the Subject line.

3. At the Add Photos dialogue box, select the photo(s) to attach, clicking Add after each.

4. Click Done when you have them all.

5. The photo will have been placed in your message, and a new set of tools will have appeared. Use these to add a border to the picture, or edit it as required.

6. To change the size of the photo, click the Layout button, then pick a different size in the layout options.

You'll know if an incoming message has an attachment as there will be a little paperclip icon beside it in the header list. If you have opted to show the message header in the Reading pane, the attachment's name will be shown there, below the To: list.

For this next exercise you need a message with an attached file. So, you can either wait until someone sends you one, or you can attach a file to a message, set it to send later – so that it is in the Outbox – and then open the message. (And don't forget to delete it later if you only created the message to test the procedure!)

Saving an attached file

1 Open the message.

2 If the Reading pane message header is present, right-click on the attachment's name and select Save As.

otherwise

3 Open the File menu and select Save Attachments.

4 Locate the folder in which to store the file, then click Save.

Timesaver tip

If a picture has been attached to an HTML formatted message, you will be able to see it. Right-click on it and select the Save Picture As… command – it's exactly the same technique as you would use for capturing an image of a web page.

4

Opening an attachment

You can open an attachment directly from a message, without saving it. But take care. Some very nasty viruses are spread through email attachments. You get a message, apparently from an acquaintance, and when you open it, the virus program is executed. Typically, it will go through your address book, sending virus-laden messages to your contacts, and it may also destroy the files on the hard drive.

Any executable file (program) may be a virus. Common extensions for executable files include: .exe, .com, .bat, .vbx. Viruses can also be hidden in macros – programs that run within applications. These can be a problem in Word, Excel and PowerPoint. If you have any of these, make sure that they are set for high security in respect of macros. Go to the Tools menu, point to Macros, select Security… and set the level to High.

1 Open the message.

2 If the Reading pane message header is present, right-click on the attachment's name and select Open.

otherwise

3 Double-click on the message to open it in its own window, then right-click on the filename in the Attach line and select Open.

4 At the Mail Attachment dialogue box, think again and if you have any doubts about the file's safety, click Cancel.

5 If you are confident that it is safe, click Open.

Important

Never open an executable file unless you have been expecting it and are absolutely certain that it is safe.

There are several ways in which you can customise your display. The first of these is to select the screen elements that you want to include in the layout. This is done in the Layout dialogue box. Simply tick or clear the ticks to turn elements on and off.

◀ **Adjusting the layout**

1 Click the Menus button and select Layout.

2 Click on the name of an area, e.g. Folder pane, to set its layout options.

3 Click to select from alternative displays …

4 … or to turn optional elements on or off.

5 Click Apply to see the effect of your changes.

6 Go back to step 2 if you don't like the new layout.

7 Click OK to return to Live Mail, or leave the dialogue box open and read on…

4

Important !

Most of these settings only affect how Live Mail looks, not how it works. The Reading pane options are different. See page 94.

Controlling the
Reading pane

The Reading pane is optional – a message can also be opened into its own window. If the pane is present, it automatically displays whatever message is selected in the Message List. This can be useful, but it can also be a cause of problems – it all depends on how good the filters are at your Internet service provider. If they are filtering out the spam and those messages that contain viruses, then the Reading pane can be used safely. If not, turn the pane off so that you control which messages are opened.

1 Click the Menus button, and select Layout.

2 In the Reading pane area, click the checkbox to turn the pane on or off.

   If the pane is on...

3 Select where the pane is to go – below is generally better as you can normally read the whole width of the message without scrolling the display.

4 Click OK.

Important

The message headers in the Reading pane repeat the details from the Message list, so are very often simply a waste of space, but they do make it easier to deal with attachments (see page 91).

Simple word processing

5

Introduction

Word processing is probably the most widely used computer application, and the most widely used word processing software is Microsoft Word. You probably have Word on your machine. It is often included in 'package deals' on new PCs, and supplied ready-installed – if yours is new, and you are still exploring it, have a look for Word now. Is it on the Programs group on the Start menu? If you cannot see a 'Microsoft Word' item on the main list, is there a 'Microsoft Office' submenu containing Word? Word is also included in some versions of the Works software suite, which is also commonly bundled with new PCs.

If you do not have Word on your PC, don't go out and buy it unless you really need its advanced facilities, as Windows comes with a perfectly good, if slightly limited, word processor. WordPad can handle letters, reports, minutes of meetings, simple brochures and newsletters, and has much the same formatting facilities as Word. It is, in effect, a cut-down version of Word, with the same commands and toolbar buttons – but just not as many of them. In this chapter, the examples and instructions are for Word, but virtually all of them apply equally well to WordPad.

Exploring the Word screen

The main part of the screen forms the working area, where you type your text and insert graphics and other objects to create your documents. Around this area are:

■ The Title bar, showing the name of the document, and carrying the usual Minimise, Maximise/Restore and Close application buttons.

■ The Ribbon holds Word's complete set of tools. These are arranged in groups, on tabs, and these four tabs are the ones that you will use most: the Home tab has the main formatting tools; the Insert tab tools are for adding pictures, tables and other objects; those on the Page Layout tab control the size and layout of pages; and the View tab gives you different ways to view your documents.

To bring a tab to the front, click on its name.

■ The scroll bars, used for moving around your document – just drag the sliders or click the arrows at the ends to scroll the display. At the bottom of the right scroll bar are buttons for moving between pages; and at the left of the bottom bar are four buttons for changing the view. Click on each of these to see the effect – Normal or Print Layout views are best for most work.

■ The ruler, showing the margins, indents and tabs. This is not present in some views.

■ The Status bar, showing where you are in the document, what language the spell checker is using, and the state of various toggle (on/off) options.

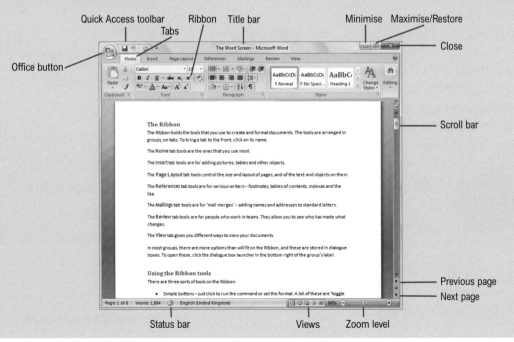

96

Using the Ribbon tools

There are three sorts of tools on the Ribbon:

■ Simple buttons – just click to run the command or set the format. A lot of these are 'toggle switches' – they turn options on or off.

■ Buttons with options – these have a little down arrow to the right. Click the arrow to open a list, and choose an option from there, or click the button to use the current default (which is normally the one you chose last time).

■ Drop-down lists – click the arrow to open the list and choose an option.

In most groups, there are more options than will fit on the Ribbon, and these are stored in dialogue boxes. To open these, click the dialogue box launcher in the bottom right of the group's label.

Toggle on/off

Dialogue box launcher

Options

Drop down list

5

Using the Microsoft Office button

There is a menu that opens from the Microsoft Office button. This holds commands which relate to the whole document – New, Open, Save, Print and the like. Some of these are simple one-job commands; others have options.

1 Click the Office button to open the menu.

2 Click a button to run the command, or click an arrow to see the options.

Start a new document

Open an existing one

Resave the document, in the same place with the same name

Save for the first time, or with a new name or in a different place

Print or preview

Check or edit the document's properties – for business users

Send by email or fax

Publish as a blog or on a company network

Close the file

Control how Word works

End the session

Word 2007 offers you five ways to look at a document.

- Print Layout shows the page as it would look when printed. This is the best view for most work.

- Full Screen Reading hides most of the controls to leave more space for reading the document.

- Web Layout is for when you are using Word to create web pages.

- Outline shows the structure of a document, as shown by its headings. We'll come back to this when we look at Styles (page 167).

- Draft just shows your text, ignoring margins and layout on the page.

Changing the view

1 Open the View tab on the Ribbon.

2 Use the tools in the Document Views group

or

3 Use the buttons on the right of the Status bar.

5

Starting a new document

All documents start from some kind of template which sets up the basic design. That bare white page that you see when you first start Word is in fact a 'blank document' template. In this case it simply sets the page size and the fonts for the normal and heading text. Other templates may have some text or images already in place – headed paper for letters, for example – and/or have more elaborate design features or suggestions for content and layout of the items to include in the new document.

Explore the templates

1 Open the Office button menu and select New.

2 Select Blank document.

3 Click Create.

or

4 In the Templates, select a category – if you choose one from Office Online, you will have to wait a few moments to see the templates.

5 Click on a template to see a preview.

6 When you find one you like, click Create.

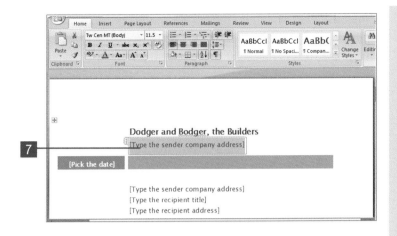

7 Click into the prompts and replace the text with your own details.

Important

Word has two typing modes: Insert and Overtype. In Insert mode, when you type into existing text the new characters push the old ones along to make room. In Overtype mode new text replaces the old. (The OVR indicator on the Status line is in bold when you are in Overtype mode.) Press the Insert key to switch between them.

5

Selecting text

To select:

■ A word – double-click anywhere in the word.

■ A line – click in the margin to the left of the line.

■ A paragraph – triple-click inside the paragraph.

■ Any other text – click at the start of the block and drag to the end.

■ Any size block – move the insertion point to the start of the block, hold down Shift and move to the end using keystrokes.

When you start typing on a blank page, the text will first appear at the top left corner and gradually fill down. In an existing document, text is placed at the insertion point – the flashing line. If this is not where you want to type, click to move the insertion point to the right place.

Before you can do any kind of editing, you must first select the text. A block of text can be any size, from one character to the whole document. How you select depends upon the size of block that you want.

Click here to select the line   You can start to select at any point

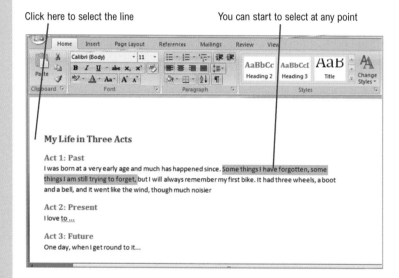

Using keys in Word

If you make a mistake, use Backspace to erase the character(s) that you have just typed.

If you spot a mistake later, click the insertion point into the text and use Backspace to erase to its left or Delete to erase to its right, or select the text and press Delete.

To move around the text using the keys:

- Arrows – one character left or right, one line up or down; one word left or right if Ctrl is held down.

- PgUp – move one screenful up.

- PgDn – move one screenful down.

- Home – jump to the start of the line; or the start of the text if Ctrl is held down.

- End – jump to the end of the line; or the end of the text if Ctrl is held down.

Selecting text (cont.)

Timesaver tip

If you want to select all the text in a document, press Ctrl and A.

Important

In Word, the cursor is an I-beam, rather than an arrow pointer. This is to help you position it more accurately in the text.

5

Editing text

When word processing, you should never have to type anything twice. If you need to use the same words several times, text can be copied. If text is in the wrong place, it can be moved.

There are two main techniques for copying and moving text.

Drag and drop

If you are reasonably competent with a mouse, this is an easy and efficient way to move or copy blocks of text.

To move a block of text

1 Select the block of text.

2 Point anywhere within the highlighted text.

3 Hold down the mouse button and move the cursor (now ⬚).

4 Release the button to drop the block into its new position.

To copy a block, follow the same steps, but hold down the Ctrl key while you drag.

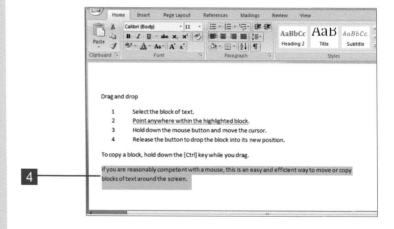

Every Windows application has the commands Cut, Copy and Paste. You will find them on the context menu that opens when you right-click on an object, and there are buttons for them in the Clipboard group on the Ribbon. These are used for copying and moving data within and between applications.

✂ Cut deletes a selected block of text, picture, file or other object, but places a copy in the Clipboard.

📋 Copy copies the selected data into the Clipboard.

📋 Paste copies the data from the Clipboard into a different place in the same application, or into a different application – as long as this can handle data in that format.

The data remains in the Clipboard until new data is copied into it, or until Windows is shut down.

To copy text

1 Select the block of text.

2 Click 📋.

or

3 Open the Edit menu or right-click and select Copy.

4 Place the cursor where you want the text.

5 Click 📋.

or

6 Right-click and select Paste.

Jargon buster

Clipboard – a special part of memory in Windows which can be used for storing any kind of data – text, images, spreadsheets, complete files or small selected chunks. It can be used not just for copying or moving data within an application, but also between applications as the Clipboard can be accessed from any program.

5

Editing text (cont.)

The Cut operation is the same as Copy except that it deletes the selected block of text, picture, file or whatever object, when it places a copy in the Clipboard.

To move text

1 Select the block of text.

2 Click ✂.

or

3 Right-click and select Cut.

4 Place the cursor where you want the text.

5 Click 📋.

or

6 Right-click and select Paste.

Timesaver tip

Word, like other programs in the Microsoft Office suite, has its own Clipboard, and this can hold up to 24 items at once – that's 23 more than the Windows Clipboard can hold! To open it, click on the launcher arrow at the bottom of the Clipboard group. You can select any item to paste, or click Paste All to copy all the items at once.

The standard Paste command pastes in the last item cut or copied.

In the old days, you were lucky if your software allowed you to undo a mistake. With Word, you can go back and undo a whole series of actions. This doesn't just protect you from your mistakes, it also gives you freedom to experiment. You can do major editing or reformatting, and if at the end you preferred things how they were, you can undo your way back to it. This is managed through the Undo button.

Redo

This is the undo-undo button! If you undid too much, use this to put it back again.

To undo one action

1 Click the arrow on the Undo button.

To undo a series of actions

2 Open the list from the Undo button.

3 Point down the list to highlight all the actions that you want to undo.

4 Click the left mouse button.

Timesaver tip

The Undo and Redo buttons are on the Quick Access toolbar. You can add to this any other commands that you use regularly. Just click the arrow on the right to open the list and select a command to add it. New, Open and Quick Print are well worth adding.

Emphasising text

You can add emphasis to text in several ways. The simplest is to make it **bold**, *italic* or underlined.

These options can be used by themselves, or in combination – this is ***bold and italic*** – to pick out words within a paragraph, to emphasise whole paragraphs or to make headings stand out more.

You can set these options using the buttons in the Font group on the Ribbon or on the mini toolbar, or using the keystroke shortcuts.

To format with buttons

1. Select the text to be formatted.
2. Click the **B** button to turn Bold on or *I* to set italics or U to underline.

To remove the formatting

3. Select the text again and click the same button to turn the effect off.

Timesaver tip

You can format text with these keystroke shortcuts:

Press Control and B to set Bold

Press Control and I to set Italic

Press Control and U to set Underline.

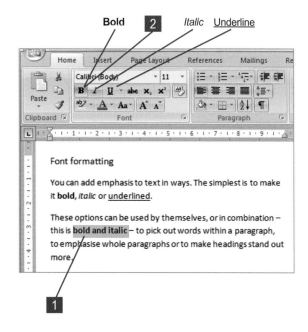

A font is a typeface design, identified by name. There are many thousands of fonts around – Windows comes equipped with several dozen.

To set the font

1 Select the text to be formatted.

2 Click the ⊡ button to the right of the font name to drop down the list – the names are set in their own fonts, so you have examples.

3 Select an option from the list.

?

Did you know?

Fonts can be grouped into four overall categories.

Serif fonts have little 'tails' (the serifs) on the end of the long strokes. They are usually very 'readable' and so are normally used for large amounts of text. Popular serif fonts include Times New Roman, Georgia and Garamond.

T   T

Serif   Sans

Sans serif fonts have simpler lines. They are often used for headings, captions, children's books and other places where small amounts of clear text are wanted. This is Arial. Other sans serif fonts include Helvetica and Tahoma.

Display fonts are those where the visual effect is more important than readability. They are mainly used for headings and in advertisements or posters, where maximum impact is needed. Some display fonts are: **Impact**, Remedy, *Calligraphy* and **S T E N C I L**.

Picture fonts are sets of special characters and images which can be 'typed' into text. They are mainly used for formulae, marking bullet lists or other special effects. Examples include αβχ©∑ (Symbol) and ☎☺☻❶❷➔ (Wingdings).

5

Changing the text size

The size of the text can be set from the drop-down list beside the Font in the Font group on the Ribbon.

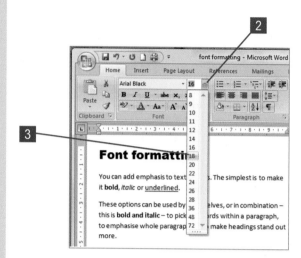

1 Select the text to be formatted.

2 Click the ▾ button to the right of the size number.

3 Select the size from the list.

Important

It is usually best to set the font before the size as some fonts are larger than others with the same nominal size. You should see how big the characters look before you set the size.

This is the simplest way to handle formatting most of the time. At first, this has a standard set of core controls but it adapts to you. Word notes which formatting tools you use most often and adds them to the toolbar. So, while they all start out the same, they gradually adapt to their users – yours may not have quite the same set of tools as this.

1 Select some text and the toolbar will appear as a ghost image.

2 Point to it, and the image firms up.

3 Click a button to apply a format.

4 Drop down the options and select from there.

Did you know?

Text size is normally measured in points. This text is 12 point. It can be any size, though you do not usually see it under 6 point or over 72 point in books or magazines.

6 point

9 point

12 point

24 point

48 point

5

Colouring your text

Word offers you two ways to colour text. You can set the font colour – the ink, as it were – or highlight the text by colouring the 'paper' behind it. There are two differences between using text colour and using highlights:

- With highlights you have a smaller choice of colours.
- The Highlight tool can be turned on so that you go through a piece highlighting lots of different words and phrases without having to reselect the tool every time.

To set the Font colour

1 Select the text.

2 Click the Font colour button to apply the current colour.

or

3 Click ⏷ beside the Font colour button.

4 Pick a colour from the palette.

To highlight text

5 Select the text.

6 Click the Highlight button to apply the current highlight colour.

or

7 Click ⏷ beside the Highlight button.

8 Pick a colour from the palette.

To turn on the highlighter

Do not select text. If any is selected already, deselect it by clicking once anywhere on the document.

Open the Highlight palette and pick a colour. The cursor will now have a little highlighter icon next to the I beam. Drag the highlighter over the text to be coloured. Repeat as required.

To return to normal editing, click once on the Highlight button.

The alignment settings control the position of text in relation to the margins. You will find the tools in the Paragraph group on the Ribbon.

The alignment options can only be applied to whole paragraphs. A paragraph is selected if any part of it is selected or it contains the insertion point.

In Word, the simplest way to set alignment is to use the toolbar buttons.

Left aligned text is flush with the left margin, but ragged on the right-hand side. It is the default in Word. This text is left aligned.

Right aligned text is flush with the right margin. A common example of its use is for the sender's address on a letter.

Centre alignment sets each line mid-way between the margins. Headings are often centred.

Justified text makes the words flush with the margins on both sides. It gives a page a neater look than left alignment, but can sometimes produce wide gaps between words.

Left Centre   Right   Justified

1 Select the paragraph(s) to be formatted. To select a single paragraph, click anywhere inside it. To select several paragraphs in a block, click anywhere inside the first, then drag the highlight down to anywhere in the last.

2 Click the appropriate toolbar button.

Timesaver tip

You can also use these keystroke shortcuts:

Press Control and L for Left alignment

Press Control and R for Right alignment

Press Control and E for Centre alignment

Press Control and J for Justified.

5

Setting the line spacing

Line spacing refers to the amount of vertical space between lines of text. The spacing can only be applied to whole paragraphs and is probably best set through the Paragraph dialogue box.

Text is normally set with single line spacing, so that there is a slim gap between the bottom of one line and the top of the next. This paragraph has single line spacing.

Double spacing is typically used where people want to leave room

between the lines for handwritten notes on the printed copy.

The line spacing can also be set to 1.5 lines or specified in

points, a measure used by printers and publishers.

1 Select the paragraph(s).

2 Click the Line spacing button.

3 Select the level from the drop-down list.

Timesaver tip

Note the other space options at the bottom of the Line Spacing list. You can use these to add a space before or after the selected paragraph(s).

114

If you are creating anything other than routine letters and memos, the Page Layout may well need changing.

Setting margins

Use the Margins options to adjust the space around the printed area. Margins should not be too small – printers can't reach the very edge of the paper and you need some white space around any text. Sometimes a slight reduction of the margins will give you a better printout. There is little more irritating than a couple of odd lines of text or a tiny block of data on a separate sheet.

If you are printing both sides of the paper, book-style, choose the Mirrored option. If they are to be ring-bound, come back to the options after setting Mirrored, choose Custom margins and then set the gutter width (the space inside the inner margin) to allow for the hidden paper.

Paper size

You will need to change the size if you are printing on envelopes or unusual paper, and should always check it when working from a template, which may have been set up for US paper size. Use this tab also to set the orientation – upright (Portrait) or sideways (Landscape).

Breaks

This needs attention with large documents that have been divided into sections – you can set where each section starts – and where you have headers and footers, and don't want the same ones on every page.

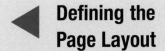

Defining the Page Layout

Did you know?

With mirror margins, the margins are Inside/Outside not Left/Right.

5

Defining the Page Layout (cont.)

1 Click the Page Layout tab on the Ribbon to bring it to the front.

2 Click the Margins button to drop down a list of options, and choose a pre-set.

3 If you need a special margin size, click Custom Margins and set the exact size in the dialogue box.

4 Set the Orientation – Portrait (the normal way) or Landscape (with the paper on its side).

5 Click the Size button and check that the right size is selected – A4 is normal in the UK.

6 If you want to start a new page or section, locate the cursor, then drop down the Breaks list and select the type of break.

There are two file-saving routines in Word, as in most Windows applications.

- <u>Save</u> is used to save an existing file after editing – just click or open the File menu and select Save.
- Save As is used to save a new file, or to save an existing file with a new name or in a new folder – see the steps.

When you Save As in Word, a filename is created for you from the first line of the document. If it is not suitable, replace it with your own.

1 Click to save a new file.

or

2 Open the Office button menu and select Save As to save a file with a new name or location.

3 Set the Save in folder.

4 Enter the Filename.

5 Change the Save as type setting if required.

6 Click Save.

7 Return to editing, or exit, as desired.

Timesaver tip

You can save in different formats if you need to transfer documents to other applications.

If the document is going to be opened by anyone who has an earlier version of Word, then save it in the Word 97–2003 format.

5

Using Print Preview

1. Click the Office button to open the menu.

2. Point to Print and select Print Preview.

3. Use the Zoom tool to get a close-up and an overview of the pages.

4. Use the Page Setup tools to adjust the page layout, if necessary.

5. Print the document from here, if it is ready,

   otherwise

6. Click Close Print Preview and go back to editing mode.

Timesaver tip

If you have an odd few lines on the last page, click Shrink One Page. This will squeeze the spacing throughout the document to try and make it fit.

If you work in Print Layout view, you can see – as you create the document – how it will fit on paper. By dropping the Zoom level down to Whole page or Two pages, you can get a better impression of the overall layout of the document.

Print Preview lets you view more pages at a time (as thumbnails), has a flexible Zoom facility, with a 100% button to switch quickly back to normal, and shows the headers and footers more clearly. When previewing, you can change the page setup or reformat selected areas using the Mini toolbar, but if the document needs any real work doing to it, you will find it simpler to return to the normal working view.

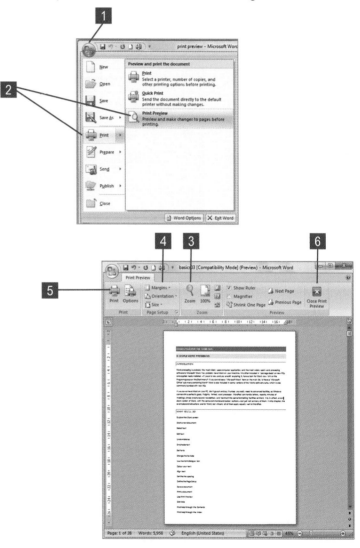

Word is WYSIWYG (What You See Is What You Get), so that what you see on screen is very close to its appearance when printed. Because of this, the Quick Print routine works well most of the time. If you want to print selected pages, or need several copies, or have other special requirements, the Print dialogue box gives you more control of the output.

◀ Printing a document

To control the printing

1 If you only want to print part of a page, select the text first.

2 Open the Office button menu, point to Print and select Print.

3 Set the range of pages to print.

4 Set the Copies number – turn on Collate to print multiple copies in sorted sets.

5 For double-sided printing, set the Print option to Odd pages, then feed the paper back in – in reverse order – and repeat with Even pages.

6 Click OK.

! Important

If you select text before starting, the Selection option will be available in the Page Range area.

5

Timesaver tip

To print one copy of the whole document, using the default printer, just click 🖨.

Getting Help

The simplest way to get Help is to ask for it. Type your question and Word will search through its Help system and offer you any topics that seem to be relevant.

If you have set up the Help options in Windows to use the online Help, then the search will include the system at Microsoft as well as the information stored in your own hard disk.

1 Click the Help icon at the top right of the Word window to open the Help window.

2 Type a question or one or more keywords in the box at the top left of the window and click Search.

3 After a moment the results will be listed, with the best matches at the top.

Important

You don't actually need to type a properly worded question – simply giving one or more key words will do the job. 'custom bullets' will produce the same results as 'How do I customise bullets in a list?'

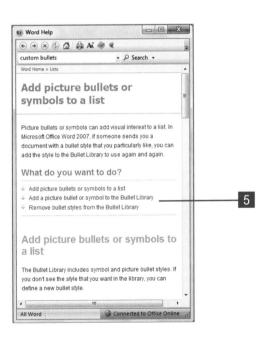

4 Click a blue link to reach the Help page.

5 Headings with a blue arrowhead beside them are sets of instructions. Click on the heading to display the instructions.

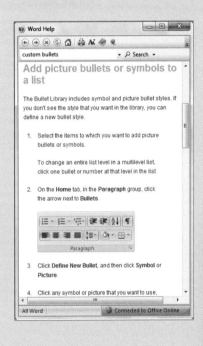

Browsing the Help system

If you are not sure which words to use to search for specific help, or if you want to browse to see what is available, have a look in the Table of Contents. Pick a heading (with a ◈ icon) and open that to see the page titles. Some sections have subsections, making it a two or three-stage process to get to page titles.

Some Help pages have a set of headings which you can open up to get detailed instructions on how to perform specific tasks.

1 Click the Help icon at the top right of the Word window to open the Help window.

2 Click the Table of Contents icon. The window will double in width, with the Table of Contents on the left and a display area on the right.

3 Click on a to open up a section.

4 Click to close a section if it is not wanted.

5 Click on a heading with a to display a Help page.

6 Words or phrases highlighted in the text in blue have explanations attached to them. Click on the word and the text will expand to display the explanation.

5

Managing your files

6

Introduction

To be able to use your computer efficiently, you must know how to manage your files – how to find, copy, move, rename and delete them – and how to organise the folders on your disks. In Windows 7, the program that is used for file management is Windows Explorer. In this chapter we will see how it can be used for file and folder management. We will also look at creating links between documents and applications, and at the Recycle Bin – a neat device which makes it much less likely that you will delete files by accident.

The hard disk is the main place for storing files, but it is not the only one. Files can also be written on floppy disks, CD/DVD ROM disks and memory sticks, for backup storage, or to move from one PC to another. We will be looking at these external storage media towards the end of the chapter.

Understanding files and folders

The hard disks supplied on modern PCs are typically 80 gigabytes or larger. 1 Gigabyte is 1 billion bytes and each byte can hold one character (or part of a number or of a graphic). That means that a typical hard disk can store nearly 16 billion words – enough for about 80,000 hefty novels! More to the point, if you were using it to store letters and reports, it could hold many, many thousands of them. Even if you are storing big audio or video files you are still going to get hundreds of them on the disk. It must be organised if you are ever to find your files.

Folders

Folders provide this organisation. They are containers in which related files can be placed to keep them together, and away from other files. A folder can also contain sub-folders – which can themselves by subdivided. You can think of the first level of folders as being sets of filing cabinets; those at the second level are drawers within the cabinets, and the next level are equivalent to divisions within the drawers. (And these could have subdividers too – there is no limit to this.)

You can just store all your files in My Documents, but it will get terribly crowded! It is a good idea to have a separate folder for each type of file, or each area of work, subdividing as necessary, so that no folder holds more than a few dozen files.

Paths

The structure of folders is often referred to as the tree. It starts at the root, which is the drive letter – C: for your main hard disk – and branches off from there.

A folder's position in the tree is described by its path. For most operations, you can identify a folder by clicking on it in a screen display, but now and then you will have to type its path. This should start at the drive letter and the root, and include every folder along the branch, with a backslash (\) between the names.

For example:

    C:\DTP
    C:\WordProcessing\Letters2007

When you want to know a path, look it up in the Explorer display and trace the branches down from the root.

Filenames

A filename has two parts – the name and an extension separated by a dot.

The name can be as long as you like, and include almost any characters – including spaces. But don't let this freedom go to your head. The longer the name, the greater the opportunity for typing errors. The most important thing to remember when naming a file is that the name must mean something to you, so that you can find it easily next time you want to use it.

The extension can be from 0 to 4 characters, and is used to identify the nature of the file. Windows uses the extensions COM, EXE, SYS, INI, DLL to identify special files of its own – handle these with care!

Most applications also have their own special extensions. Word files are often DOCX or DOC; spreadsheet files are usually XLSX or XLS; database files typically have DB extensions.

If you are saving a file in a word processor, spreadsheet or other application, and are asked for a filename, you only have to give the first part. The application will take care of the extension.

Libraries

A library looks like a folder, but is in fact a set of links to one or more folders, that may be scattered throughout your system. The purpose of libraries is to bring stuff together for ease of access. My Pictures library, for example, has My Picture folder, the Public Pictures folder, and another folder of photos that is stored elsewhere on the C: drive. I can also add to it my camera's own storage, and other folders on my PC and on other PCs in the local network. If I want to do anything with all my pictures, such as backing

them up, or selecting a set for printing or publishing, or whatever, I only need to go to the Pictures Library.

Important

If there are several users, they will each have their own 'My Documents' folder set up by Windows 7 – any new folders should be created within this.

This is my Pictures folder. Most of my pictures are stored in the three folders: *basic*, *France* and *Vista*, but you will see a few unfiled images too.

Browsing for files

Don't worry too much about remembering paths. When you want to access a file in an application, you will usually be taken to an Open dialogue box in which you can select the drive, folder and file from a graphical display. Those that do not open this dialogue box directly will have a Browse button to open it.

Browsing dialogue boxes from two applications.

Important

In some older applications 'folders' are called 'directories'.

Jargon buster

Root – the folder of the disk. All other folders branch off from the root.
Parent – a folder that contains another.
Child – a sub-folder of a Parent.
Branch – the structure of sub-folders that opens off from a folder.

Unlike every other Windows application, Windows Explorer (or Explorer for short) does not have its name in the title bar, and it is rarely started by name. The title bar displays the path to the folder that is open in Explorer, and the normal way of starting it is to open a folder.

The Explorer display can be varied in several ways. Some elements can be turned on or off, and some change in response to the material that is currently displayed. These four are always present:

■ The Current Folder box shows you where you are now.

■ The Search box can be used to hunt for a file (see page 156).

■ The Toolbar buttons vary according to the type of folder or file that is selected at the time.

■ The Contents pane usually shows the contents of the current folder. For Computer it shows the disks and other storage on the PC.

These are optional, though the first two are normally present:

■ The Navigation pane lists the libraries, folders and drives on your system. Use this to change the current folder.

■ The Details pane tells you the size, date and other details about the selected file or folder.

■ The Preview pane shows a small version of an image or the first page of other documents, if a preview is available.

■ The Search pane opens up when you run an advanced search.

■ The Menu bar gives another way to reach the commands and options. It is normally hidden. To display it, press the Alt key.

If it has been turned on, the Status bar lies at the bottom of the window and shows the number of objects in the folder or the size of a selected file.

Exploring Windows Explorer

To start Explorer

1 Click the Start button.

2 Click Computer in the links on the right-hand side. This will run Explorer and open the Computer folder, which holds all the disk drives on your system.

Current Folder box

Contents pane

Menu bar

Toolbar

Search box

Navigation pane

Details pane

Preview pane

Customising the layout

To turn the optional panes and Menu bar on or off:

1. Click on the Organise button.

2. Point to Layout.

3. Click on an element to toggle its display.

   If you turn on the Preview pane in Computer, there will be nothing to see. Let's find something else.

4. Click Pictures in the Favourite Links list. Check that the Preview pane is present – it may not be, as Explorer opens each folder with the same display as was used previously. Turn it on if necessary.

5. Select a file and see if it has a preview.

6. The preview will be scaled to fit the Preview pane. If you want to change the size of the pane, drag on the divider.

Timesaver tip

Click the Preview pane button on the toolbar to toggle the Preview pane on and off.

Explorer can display files and folders in five views – List, Content, Details, Tiles and Icons, and the icons can be anything from Small to Extra Large. The display is controlled through the Views button.

The Icons view shows a thumbnail of each file, if it can, and otherwise an icon to identify its type. It works best with images, but documents with previews can also be thumbnailed. The icons and thumbnails can be as large as you need to be able to identify files.

The List view is similar to Small Icons view, but packs more files into the same screen space.

Details gives a column display of properties under the headings Name, Type, Size, Tags, Date modified and others (these vary – see page 134). Every file has properties. Some of these are set by the system, e.g. its type and size; others can be changed by you, such as its name and where it is stored. Some properties are common to all types of files, but some types have additional properties.

Tiles displays a medium icon for each file, plus its name and other essential details.

Contents view is similar to Tiles, but displaying a little more information.

To change the view

1 Click the Views button to cycle between the main types.

or

2 Click the arrow beside the Views button to see the options.

3 Click on a name to select a view.

or

4 Drag the slider to adjust the size – you can stop part-way between two set views to get an intermediate size.

Viewing files (cont.)

Common file icons

 Bitmap image

 Web page

 Text

 Word document

 Excel workbook

 Open Type font

 System file – handle with care!

 Movie file

 Zip compressed file

Tile view

Did you know?

When an option can be turned on and off by clicking on it in a menu, this is known as a toggle switch.

For your information

Image icons are normally replaced by thumbnails of the image.

Details view

List view

Medium icons view

Content View

Timesaver tip

If you turn on the Menu bar, you will have some additional layout and view options.

Customising the headings

You can choose which properties to include in the headings. This determines the properties that are displayed in Details view, but also affects the way that you can sort and group files in any view – see page 131.

To customise the headings

1. Right-click anywhere along the headings. The menu lists the more important properties.

2. Click on a property name to toggle the tick on or off.

3. If you can't see the property you want to include, click More…

4. At the Choose Details dialogue box, tick the details you want to include.

5. The order of the columns in the display matches the order in this list. Select a detail and use the Move Up and Move Down buttons to rearrange its order if required.

6. Click OK.

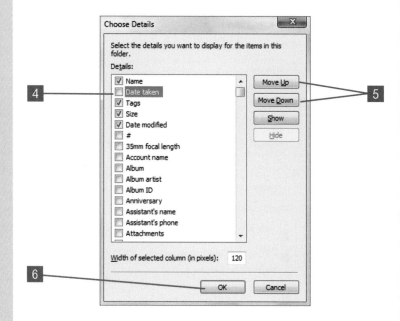

The Navigation pane gives you an easy way to switch between folders, and to move files between them. It shows the disk drives, folders and network connections in a branching structure.

1 If the Navigation pane is not open, set the Layout options to display it.

2 Click on any folder to select it. Its files and subfolders will be listed in the main pane.

3 A ▷ icon to the left of a folder name shows that the folder has subfolders. Click this to open up the branch.

4 The icon changes to ◢ . Click this to close the branch.

Creating a folder

Organised people set up their folders before they need them, so that they have places to store their letters – private and business – reports, memos, notes, and whatever, when they start to write them on their new system. They have a clear idea of the structure that they want, and create their folders at the right branches.

1 In the Navigation pane, select the folder that will be the parent of your new one, or the root if you want a first level folder.

2 The toolbar will now have a New Folder button – click it.

3 Replace 'New Folder' with a new name – any length, any characters, as with filenames.

Important

Which display you use for your file management is up to you. I prefer to see the folder structure for most jobs – certainly for organising files and folders – but I sometimes turn off the Navigation pane when I'm simply looking to see what's where or if I need two folders open at once to compare their contents.

Timesaver tip

If you want to change the name of a folder, right-click on it and select Rename, or use Rename this folder from the Common Tasks display.

Organised people may set up their folders before they create the documents that will go into them, but the rest of us set up our new folders when the old ones get so full that it is difficult to find things. Nor do we always create them in the most suitable place in the tree. Fortunately, Windows 7 caters for us too. Files can easily be moved from one folder to another, and folders can easily be moved to new places on the tree.

Here, Holiday photos is being moved from within My Documents into My Pictures, where it really belongs.

1 Arrange the display so that you can see the folder you want to move and the place it has to move to.

2 Drag the folder to its new position – the highlight will show you which one is currently selected.

See also

Moving and copying files, page 150.

Timesaver tip

Copying a folder – and all its files – to another disk can be a quick way to make a backup of a set of files.

Setting the folder type

Windows can be set to handle folders in slightly different ways if they hold pictures, sound or video files. This will affect the Tasks display – unless you have replaced these by Folders – and the default View setting.

1 In the Navigation pane or the main display, right-click on the folder.

2 Select Properties.

3 On the Customise tab pick a folder type to suit the contents.

Change the picture

4 If you want to change the image on the front of the folder, click Choose File... and browse for one.

Change the icon

5 If you want to change the icon used for the folder by Windows Explorer, click Change Icon...

6 Select the most suitable icon.

7 Click OK.

8 Back at the Properties dialogue box, click OK to save your settings.

These control the overall appearance of folders and the way that files are handled. The dialogue box has three tabs.

On the General tab there are three options:

- You can open each folder in a new window or in the same one.
- You can select items with a single or double-click.
- You can tweak how the Navigation pane displays folders.

The View panel controls the display of files. There are two main options here. The first is whether to show 'hidden' files. These are mainly found in the Windows and Windows/System folders. They are ones that you do not usually need to see and which are safer out of the way.

- Application extensions – files with .DLL extensions. They are used by applications and must not be deleted.
- System files – marked by .SYS after the name. These are essential to Windows' internal workings.
- Drivers – with .VXD or .DRV extensions. These make printers, screens and other hardware work properly.

The second key choice is whether you want to set different display styles for different folders – turn on Remember each folder's view settings if you do. If you have a mixture of styles already and want all folders to look the same, you can use the buttons to make them all look like the current folder or reset them all to their default settings.

The Search tab controls how Windows searches for files.

Setting Folder Options (cont.)

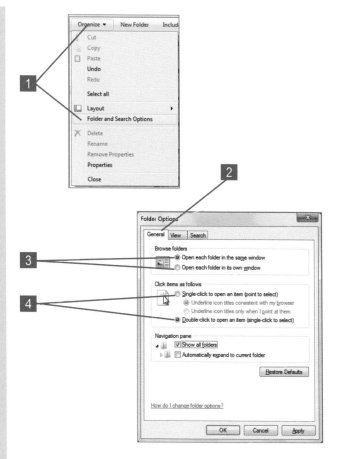

1. Click on the Organise button and select Folder and Search Options.

2. Start on the General tab.

3. Set the Browse Folders option – the same or a new window?

4. Set the Click option.

5. Go to the View panel.

6. Click the checkbox to turn options on or off.

7. Click Apply to test the effect.

8. Click OK.

! Important

You can change the options when and as often as you like.

If you want the same folder display throughout, click a button to use the current or the default settings

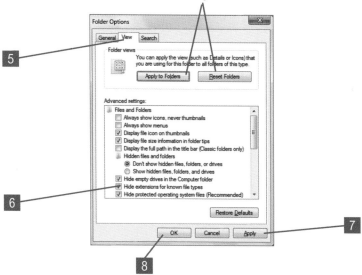

On the Search tab you can specify what, how and when to search. Windows creates indexes for your documents, based on the author, tags, and other properties. The default search routine looks through these indexes, and through the names of non-indexed files (mainly those of application and system programs).

1 In What to search, you can extend a search so that it also looks through the text of documents – very thorough, but rather slow, or restrict it to filenames – faster but you have to know some or all of the name.

2 In How to search, the key option is probably Find partial matches. If this is on, the search can find files based on a few letters of a name or tag – but note that this may find lots of irrelevant files that match those few letters.

3 In When searching non-indexed locations, you would not normally want to search the system folders, but if you have stored documents in compressed folders to save space, you may well want to search them.

Adding to a library

Windows comes with ready-made libraries for Documents, Music, Pictures and Videos, and these will all include folders of the same names in your storage area, and in the Public area. You can add more folders or remove ones that you do not want, and create new libraries if needed.

1 In the Navigation pane, select a library or any of the folders in it.

2 On the left of the headers is a button marked 'library locations' – click it.

3 The dialogue box lists the locations in the library. Click the Add button.

4 Navigate through your system to find the folder that you want to include in the library.

5 Click Include folder.

6 If you no longer want a folder in the library, select it and click Remove.

The files in a library are normally listed by folder, but can be arranged in different ways. The choice of ways depends upon the type of files stored in it; for example, in the Documents library files can be arranged by name, author, type, date and tag.

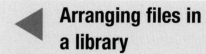
1 In the headers, click the button to the right of Arrange by.

2 Click on the property to arrange by.

Important

If you want to create a library, find the top-level Libraries in the Navigation pane, right-click on it, point to New and select Library, then edit the new library's name.

Using tags

Tags are a type of property that can be used to sort, filter and group files in Explorer displays. They are handy for classifying digital photos, but they can help in any situation where a file can fit into several categories.

To add tags

1 Make sure that the Details pane is present in Explorer.

2 Select the file.

3 In the Details pane, click where it says Tags: Add a tag.

4 If this is the first time you have used the tag, type it in.

5 To add another tag, type a semicolon (;). Add a tag will reappear, and you can type in more.

6 Tags are stored by the system. If you want to add a tag that you have already used for other files, type the first letter or two. Any that contain the same letters will be listed below the Tags box – click one to select. It will be written in for you and 'Add a tag' will appear at the end again.

7 Press Enter or click Save to end.

8 If you want to remove a tag, select the file and click into the Tags box in the Details pane.

9 You cannot edit tags. If you decide one is not right, you must delete it and type a new one.

Important

Not all types of files can take tags. For example, you can add them to JPGs (the standard digital photo format) but not to text files, BMP images or web pages. If it doesn't say Tags in the Details pane, the file can't take them.

Explorer allows you to display files in groups. The groups can be based on any property shown in the headings, so you can group by type, or date, or tags. Tags have a unique effect on groups – if a file has more that one tag, it will be included in every matching group. This increases the number of items on display, but the grouping makes it simpler to find the ones you want.

To group files

1 Right-click in the Contents display, anywhere on the background – not on a file or folder.

2 Point to Group By.

3 Select the property to use.

To clear the grouping

4 Right-click anywhere on the background.

5 Point to Group By and select None.

Sorting files

▶

Unless you specify otherwise, folders and files are listed in alphabetical order. Most of the time this works fine, but when you are moving or copying files, or hunting for them, other arrangements can be more convenient. You can sort them into order of name, type, size or the date that they were last used.

To sort files

 Open the View menu and point to Sort By.

 Select Name, Size, Type, or Date modified.

or in Details view

3 To sort by Name, Size, Type or Date, click on the column header.

4 Click on the header again to sort into reverse order.

Timesaver tip

If the Menu bar is not displayed, right-click in the Content pane and select Sort By from the pop-up menu.

When you drop down the menu from a property heading, you will see the way files can be grouped – a list of tags or file types, alphabetical or size ranges, or whatever is appropriate to the property. You can use these same criteria to filter the display, so that only those files from selected groups are shown.

Filtering only works in Details view.

To filter files

1 Click the down arrow on the property you want to use.

2 Tick those groups that you want to include – the display will change to show the selected ones and hide the rest.

3 Click anywhere off the menu to close it.

4 To restore the display so that all the files are included, you can either tick every box in the list or clear the ticks from them all – do which ever takes the fewest clicks!

?

Did you know?

Obviously names are unique, so you can't use them for grouping – instead files are grouped by alphabetical ranges. In the same way, size ranges can be used for grouping.

Selecting files

You can easily select one file by clicking on it, but you can also select sets of files. This is useful when you want to back up a day's work, by copying the new files to a disk, or move a set from one folder to another or delete a load of unwanted files.

You can select:

- a block of adjacent files
- a scattered set
- the whole folder-full.

The same techniques work with all display styles.

To select a block using the mouse

1 Point to one corner of the block and click.

2 Drag an outline over the ones you want.

To Shift select

3 Click on the file at one end of the block.

4 If necessary, scroll the window to bring the other end into view.

5 Hold Shift.

6 Click on the far end file.

Timesaver tip

It may be easier to arrange icons by Name, Date or Type, before you start to select.

148

Selecting files (cont.)

6 in top right.

6

To select scattered files

7 Click on any one of the files you want.

8 Hold Control and click on each of the other files.

9 You can deselect any file by clicking on it a second time.

To select all the files

10 Click on the Organise button.

11 Choose Select All.

Timesaver tip

If you have the Menu bar displayed and you want all the files except for a scattered few, select those few, then use Edit, Invert Selection to deselect them and select the others.

Moving and copying files

1 Select the file(s).

2 Scroll the Folders list so that you can see the target folder – don't click on it!

3 Point to any one of the selected files and drag to the target.

or

4 Hold down the right mouse button while you drag then select Move or Copy.

Timesaver tip

The easiest way to copy a file to a disk is to right-click on it to open its Context menu, then point to Send To and select the disk drive.

When you drag a file from one place to another, the file will either move or be copied. In general:

■ It moves if you drag it to somewhere on the same disk.
■ It is copied if you drag the file to a different disk.

When you are dragging files within a disk, you are usually moving to reorganise your storage; and copying is most commonly used to create a safe backup on a separate disk.

If you want to move a file from one disk to another, or copy within a disk, hold down the right mouse button while you drag. A menu will appear when you reach the target folder. You can select Move or Copy from there.

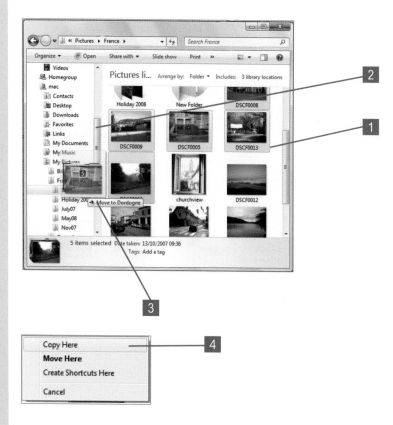

If you are having difficulty arranging the Explorer display so that you can see the source files and the target folder, the simplest approach is to use the Move To Folder or Copy To Folder commands. These let you pick the target folder through a dialogue box.

Move To Folder/Copy To Folder

5 If the Menu bar is not displayed, open it now.

6 Select the file(s).

7 Open the Edit menu.

8 Select Copy To or Move To Folder.

9 Select the target drive or folder.

10 Click Move or Copy.

Timesaver tip

You can use the Cut, Copy and Paste commands to move and copy files and folders. Find them on the Edit menu, or on the Context menu when you right-click on a file or in a folder.

Copy stores a copy of the file or folder in the Clipboard.

Cut removes the original file, storing a copy in the Clipboard.

Paste puts a copy of the stored file into the current folder.

Managing your files 151

Renaming files

You can rename a file if necessary – and it may well be necessary if the original name was created automatically by a program, as happens when you import images from a digital camera into the PC.

1 Select the file you want to rename.

2 Press F2 on your keyboard.

or

3 Click on the Organise button or open the right-click menu and select Rename.

4 Edit the name as required and press Enter to fix the new name.

Important

When renaming files, do not change their extensions! If you do, you will lose the document–application link.

In the earlier days of computing, it was all too easy to delete a file by mistake, wiping out hours or days – or even weeks – of work. Windows protects you from yourself! When you delete a file, it is not immediately erased from the hard disk. Instead it is taken from its folder and placed in the Recycle Bin, from which it can easily be recovered.

1 Select the file, or group of files.

2 Right-click and select Delete.

or

3 Press Delete.

4 At the Confirm prompt, click Yes or No to confirm or stop the deletion. With single deletions, the filename is displayed; with multiple deletions you just get the number of selected files.

Important

Floppy disks and memory sticks are different from hard disks. If you delete a file from a floppy it really does get wiped out!

Using the Recycle Bin

To restore files

1 Open the Recycle Bin from the icon on the desktop or from Windows Explorer.

2 Select the files that were deleted by mistake – the Original Location field shows you where they were.

3 Right-click for the Context menu and select Restore or click Restore the items in the toolbar.

To empty the bin

4 Check that there is nothing that you want, and restore any files if necessary.

5 Select Empty the Recycle Bin from the toolbar.

This is a wonderful feature, especially for those of us given to making instant decisions that we later regret. Until you empty the Bin, any 'deleted' files and folders can be instantly restored – and if the folder that they were stored in has also been deleted, that is re-created first, so things go back into their proper place.

Files sent to the Recycle Bin stay there until you empty it. You should do this regularly, to free up disk space.

Timesaver tip

You can delete folders or files by dragging them directly to the Recycle Bin.

This is not something you will do every day, for deleting a folder also deletes its files, and files are usually precious things. But we all acquire programs we don't need, keep files long past their use-by dates, and sometimes create unnecessary folders.

1 Select the folder.

2 Check the files list. Are there any there? Do you want any of them? No, then carry on.

3 Right-click on the folder to open the Context menu or click the Organise button and select Delete.

4 If necessary, you can stop the process by clicking No when you are asked to confirm that the folder is to be thrown in the Bin.

Important

If you delete a folder by mistake it can be restored from the Recycle Bin.

Finding files

Windows Explorer has a neat Search routine, which can track down lost files for you, hunting for them by any word or phrase in their title, text, tags or other properties.

You do not need to give the whole of the name or whatever text you are searching for. If you've mislaid your essay on Henry VIII, a search for 'hen' would find it – but it would also find every other 'henry' as well as every occurrence of 'then', 'when', 'Carmarthen', 'hen party', etc. The more specific you are in your search, the fewer results there will be for you to sort through.

To find files

1 In the Navigation pane, select the highest level folder that you think it could be in. The search routine will go through all the subfolders.

2 Click into the Search box and type all or part of the name or of a significant word. Almost as soon you start to type, the search results will be displayed in the Contents pane. Type more of the filename, and the results will be filtered further, reducing the number of matching files.

3 Double-click on the file to open it, or make a note of its folder so that you can find it easily again later.

If the search returns too many results, you can filter them by specifying the date that they were last modified, or their size – and in both cases you can give a range of values.

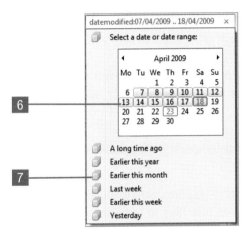

To filter by date modified

4 Click into the Search box. A short list should drop down, showing search terms you have used.

5 Click Date modified at the bottom of the list.

6 Click on the calendar to select a single day, or click on the first possible day, hold down Shift and click on the last day.

or

7 Select a time frame from the list.

Timesaver tip

When filtering by size is done, you select an approximate size range from a list.

Writing to a CD

1 In Windows Explorer, locate the files you want to write to the CD.

2 Place a blank or part-used CD in the drive. Wait for Windows to read the disk. You may be asked what you want Windows to do. The answer is to burn files to disk.

CDs come in three varieties:

A CD-ROM is read-only memory. You can read data from this kind of CD, but you cannot write it onto it. Applications software is normally supplied on CD-ROM nowadays.

A CD-W disk is writeable – you can store data on it. But this is a one-off thing. Once you have written data onto it, you cannot change what is stored there, or add more data.

A CD-R disk is rewriteable – you can store data on it, but you can add more data later, or update the files stored there. The only limitation is this: writing really is a once-only process – it changes the surface of the disk irredeemably. When you erase something from the disk, or replace a file with a newer copy, you cannot reuse the space which had been occupied by the old file. With reuse, a CD-R gradually fills up.

At the start of the Burn routine, Windows will ask you if you want to use the disk 'like a Flash USB drive', or 'with a CD/DVD player'.

- Choose Flash drive, for temporary/changeable storage on a CD-R disk.

- Choose CD/DVD player if you are burning a disk for permanent storage or to give files to someone else, e.g. for taking photos to the shop for printing.

3 Enter a title for the disk.

4 Choose how you want to use the disk – as a Flash drive, or a permanent burn.

5 You may be asked to confirm that you want to format the disk – you do. It will take a few moments.

6 A second Explorer window will open, showing the CD drive. Drag files from the first Explorer window and drop them in here. You can move them one at a time, or in groups – whichever is easiest.

7 In the Explorer window for the removable drive, click the Eject button. Wait a moment, and the disk will be ejected.

Did you know?

Most new PCs can also write to DVDs in exactly the same way as they can to CDs. Since they can store far more – 6 or 7 Gigabytes, rather than 700 Megabytes – you would normally only use them for backing up the whole system, or for storing video files.

Using a Flash drive

A Flash drive is one of the simplest and most convenient ways of storing files or transferring them between machines. In use they behave exactly like a hard drive – you can save to them, open from them and move files to and from them just as you can with any other drive. There is just one special thing about them: when you remove them, you must ensure that their files are safe first.

Every disk has a chunk of main memory linked to it, and when a file is 'written to disk' the new version may actually be in the memory and will only be copied onto the disk when the file is closed – it speeds up Save operations. So, you must make sure that files are fully written before removing the Flash drive – don't worry! It's simple to do.

1. Locate the Safely Remove Hardware icon in the area on the right of the Taskbar – it may be in the overflow window that pops up from the arrow. Click on it.

2. Select the drive that you want to remove.

3. Wait for the 'Safe to Remove Hardware' message to appear.

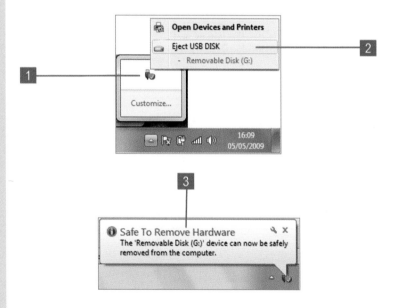

Further word processing

Introduction

You can do so much more with Word than simply type and edit text. Word has full page layout facilities – so much so that people sometimes use it to produce books. (Though in truth, it's not the software that most typesetters use if they have any choice!) But it is regularly used to produce newsletters, brochures, greetings cards, menus, advertisements and all manner of documents where appearance and style matter.

In this chapter we will explore some of Word's more advanced formatting and layout facilities. Try them out. Some you will never use again, but some you will find very handy.

And do check out the mail merge. You can save yourself a lot of time and effort next Christmas if you use mail merge to produce the labels for the cards' envelopes – or even, dare I suggest it, to personalise that 'roundup of the year' that you send out with the cards.

What you'll do

Formatting with the Font dialogue box

If you want to set several font options at the same time – perhaps to make a heading larger, bold and in a different font – or you want to set one of the less-used options, you can use the Font dialogue box. Here's how.

1 Select the text to be formatted.

2 Click the dialogue box launcher on the Font group.

3 At the Font dialogue box, make sure that you are on the Font tab.

4 Set the font, style, size and/or other options as required.

5 Check the Preview and adjust the settings if necessary.

6 Click OK.

Timesaver tip

The Character Spacing options set the spacing between letters or their vertical position. They are not often used.

Line spacing refers to the amount of vertical space between lines of text. The default is for single spacing, which is fine for most purposes. If you need more space, either to create a particular visual effect or to leave room for people to add notes on the printout, then it can be set to 1.5 lines, double spacing or other specific settings.

Using the tool in the Paragraph group, you can set the spacing to 1.15, 1.5, 2.5 or 3.0, but you can also set to any value at all through the Paragraph dialogue box.

Setting the line spacing

1 Select the paragraph(s)

2 Drop down the Line spacing list and select the level.

or

3 Click the Line Spacing options to open the Paragraph dialogue box.

4 Select Exactly from the Line Spacing options.

5 Set the gap in points.

6 Click OK.

7

Important

Line spacing can only be applied to whole paragraphs. Remember that a paragraph is selected if any part of it is selected or it contains the insertion point.

Timesaver tip

You can also open the Paragraph dialogue box from the launcher in the Ribbon.

Indenting text

Indents set the distance from the edge of the page margins of your text. They can also be used to create a structure of headings and subheadings.

The left indent can be set with the toolbar buttons – each click pushes the text in (or out) 6.3mm (0.25 in). If you want to indent from the right, or set a different left indent on the first line, you need to use the Paragraph dialogue box.

1 Select the text.

2 Click [icon] to increase the indent.

or

3 Click [icon] to pull back out.

or

4 Click the launcher to open the Paragraph dialogue box.

5 Go to the Indents and Spacing tab.

6 Type values, or use the scroll arrows to set the Left and/or Right indents.

7 To set a different indent for the first line, drop-down the Special list and select First Line or Hanging, then set the distance.

8 Click OK.

Though Indents can be set more accurately by typing values into the Indents and Spacing tab of the Paragraph dialogue box, it is quicker and simpler to use the indent markers on the ruler.

Setting indents with the ruler

9 If the ruler is not visible, switch to the View tab on the Ribbon, and in the Show/Hide group, turn on the Ribbon.

10 To set the right indent, point anywhere on the right triangle and drag into position.

11 To set the left indent, drag on the lower left triangle.

12 To set the first line indent, drag on the upper left triangle.

13 To move the left and first line indents together, drag on the square beneath the left indent triangle.

Setting tabs

If you are writing a price list, CV or similar, where text or figures need to be in accurate columns, you should use tabs.

By default, the tabs are at ½ inch (1.2 cm) intervals and left aligned. The position and the style of the tabs can be easily changed.

When you press Tab, the insertion point moves to the next tab position, pushing any existing text across with it.

Tab styles

L   Left edge of the text aligns with the tab.

┴   Text centres on the tab.

┘   Right edge of the text aligns with the tab.

⊥   Decimal points align with the tab.

I   Bar tab draws a vertical line at the tab point.

1 If the ruler is not visible, switch to the View tab on the Ribbon, and in the Show/Hide group, turn on the Ribbon.

2 Select the text for which you want to set tabs.

3 The current tab style is shown at the left of the ruler. To change the style, keep clicking the icon until you see the style you want.

4 Click on the ruler to place the tab. The default ½ inch interval tabs to its left will be removed.

5 To move a tab, click on it and drag it into a new position.

6 Repeat steps 3 to 5 to set any other tabs for the selected block of text.

7 Click anywhere in the working area to deselect the text.

A style is a combination of font, size, alignment and indent options. Word has a range of pre-defined styles, and you can modify these or add your own. Applying a style is a matter of a couple of clicks; creating a new style is almost as simple.

More

New Styles

Working with styles

To apply a style

7

1 Select the text – normally one or more whole paragraphs.

2 Select a style from the selection in the Styles group – use the up arrow to scroll the lower rows into view or click the More button for a larger display.

or

3 Click the launcher to open the pane for easier access to the set.

4 Point to a possible style and check the Live Preview to see if that is the effect you want.

5 Click on a style to apply it.

Important

Most styles are intended to be applied to whole paragraphs; others are 'character styles' which are designed for use with selected pieces of text.

Important

If you don't like any of the styles, or want a different look for the whole document, click the Change Styles button and select a new style set, colour or font set.

Working with styles (cont.)

To modify a style

6 Right-click on the style in the Styles group or pane and select Modify.

7 Edit the main formatting settings as required.

8 For more extensive changes, click the Format button and select an aspect to open its dialogue box.

9 Click OK.

To create a style

10 Click the launcher to open the Styles pane and click the New style button at the bottom left.

11 Type in a Name for the new style.

12 Select the Style type – normally either 'Paragraph' or 'Character'.

13 Select a style to base it on, if one is suitable.

14 Carry on from step 7, as above.

168

You can quickly add numbers or bullets to each item in a list by clicking the Bullets or Number tool in the Paragraph group. This will set the default bullet or number style, but other styles are readily available if you want to give your list a special look.

Here is how to apply bullets to a list. Numbers are applied in almost exactly the same way.

To add or remove bullets

1 Select the list.

2 Click the Bullets tool. If it already has bullets, this will remove them.

To add special bullets

3 Click the down arrow on the Bullet button.

4 Select a style from the Bullet Library.

or

5 Select Define new bullet ...

6 Click Symbol to choose a different character.

7

Using bullets and numbers (cont.)

7. Select a font and subset (if required).

8. Select a character.

9. Click OK.

Important

Word may be set to produce numbered or bulleted lists automatically – these are AutoFormatting options. See page 175.

Timesaver tip

You can use an image as a bullet – small, bright and distinctive work best. Click Picture in the Define New Bullet dialogue box to select the image file.

Headers and footers appear at the top and bottom of every page. They can display the page number, date and time, filename, author and similar file details, or any typed text.

The page number, date, and other details can be produced by field codes. These are replaced by the appropriate information when inserted into the pages, and are updated as necessary. For example, the Page # field code produces the correct page number on each page.

The header and footer have tabs in place so that items can go on the left, centre or right.

1 Bring the Insert tab to the front of the Ribbon and click either Header or Footer.

2 Select a style from the drop-down list.

3 Select the [Type text] placeholder where you want to add text or a field and type your text.

To insert a field

4 Go to the point on the header/footer where you want it to appear, and …

5 Click Date & Time in the Insert group and choose a style to add the date and/or time of printing.

6 Click Quick Parts and select from the list to add the author, company name or other document property or field.

7 Click Page Number, then select Current Position to add the number for each page.

8 Click Close Header and Footer when you have finished.

Timesaver tip

When you are working on the header or footer, if you select Top of Page or Bottom of Page for the page number, this will replace the current header or footer.

Checking your spelling

Word, like all modern applications that handle text, has a spell checker that compares your words with those in its dictionary. Word comes supplied with a good dictionary, but it does not cover everything. Proper names, technical and esoteric words may not be recognised and so will be classed as 'errors'. These can be added to your own custom dictionary, so that they are not seen as errors in future.

Word has a Check spelling as you type option. You may prefer to just run a spell check after you have finished – especially if you have a lot to do and need to watch the keyboard rather than the screen!

1 If you want to check part of a document, select it before starting the spell check.

2 Bring the Review tab to the front of the Ribbon and click the Spelling & Grammar tool.

When a word is not in the dictionary you can

3 Select a suggestion from the list and click Change.

   or

4 If it is a valid word click Ignore Once or Ignore All.

   or

5 Click Add to Dictionary to put it in a custom dictionary.

   or

6 Click in the Not in Dictionary slot, and edit the word then click on Change.

Timesaver tip

If you haven't already set up a dictionary for your own special words, click the Options button to reach the Spelling section of the Options and use the Custom Dictionaries button.

Word can check the grammar of a document as well as its spelling, and for both spelling and grammar there are a number of options that you can set to adjust the way they work. Probably the key option is whether or not to check as you type – some people will find that it interrupts their flow.

To set Spelling options

1. In the Spelling and Grammar dialogue box, click Options.

2. The Word Options window will open, at the Proofing section.

3. The first set of options apply to all Microsoft Office programs, and tell the checker what sort of things to ignore. Click to turn these on or off as required.

4. The second are specific to Word and control when and how the checker works. Click to toggle them on or off.

5. In the Writing Style field, the Grammar and Style option gives more guidance on style.

6. Click OK when you have done.

7

Did you know?

Word can tell you the 'readability' level of a document. A readability of Grade 7 (a reading age of 12) is a good level for an adult audience – any lower is patronising, but higher is hard work for most people. The *Daily Mail* newspaper has a reading age of 12; the *Sun's* reading age is around 8.

Timesaver tip

You can also reach the Spelling options through the Office button menu. Click the Word Options button at the bottom and select Proofing in the category list.

Correcting errors automatically

Word likes to be helpful. You can get it to watch your typing and correct some common errors as they occur. For instance, I routinely type 'hte' when I mean 'the', but Word knows what I mean and it will replace my mistyped text with the correct word as soon as I have finished it. (Which means that I have to trick it if I actually want to write 'hte'.)

You can select which sorts of errors to correct, and add your own common typos to its list of corrections.

1 Open the Office button menu and click the Word Options button at the bottom and select Proofing in the category list.

2 Click the AutoCorrect Options button.

3 On the AutoCorrect tab, tick those checkboxes where you want Word to make the correction.

4 If you turn on Replace as you type, you can add your own typos. Put the expected typo in the Replace field, and what you want to replace it with in the With field.

5 Click Add.

6 Click OK.

Timesaver tip

If there are any long names or phrases which you use regularly, e.g. the name of your football team, you could add them to your AutoCorrect list, using initials or shortforms in the Replace field. Then next time you are writing a letter to a chum complaining about their performance at the last match, you could just type WW each time instead of Wolverhampton Wanderers (or whatever).

Word can also reformat things properly as you type. For example, it can turn fractions typed like this 1/2 into special fraction characters like this ½. Or when you start to type a numbered list, it can take over the numbering for you after the first line. The options are on the AutoFormat As You Type tab of the AutoCorrect dialogue box.

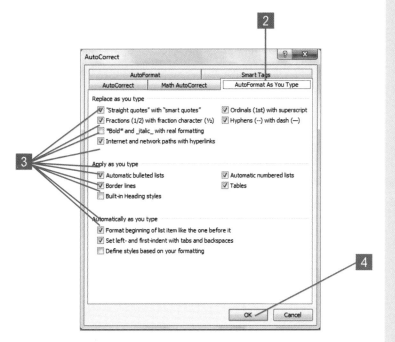

1. Open the AutoCorrect dialogue box (see page 174).

2. Switch to the AutoFormat As You Type tab.

3. Tick those checkboxes where you want Word to apply formatting as you type, or to replace characters as they are typed.

4. Click OK.

7

Applying borders and shading

Borders and shading can be very good ways to emphasise items in a document. They are normally applied to whole paragraphs, though there is nothing to stop you adding a border or a background shade – or both – to a word or phrase within a paragraph.

Borders can be applied and formatted using the options on the Borders and Shading tool – but note that you must set the formats first. You can change the formatting after the border is in place using the Borders and Shading dialogue box. This has some additional formatting options.

To add a border

1 Select the text or paragraph(s).

2 Click the drop-down arrow to the right of the Borders and Shading tool.

3 Select the Borders and Shading dialogue box.

4 Choose a Setting – Box, Shadow or 3-D.

5 Set the Line style, Colour and Weight.

6 If you only want to apply the border to selected edges, click on the unwanted borders in the Preview area to remove them.

7 Click OK.

To remove a border

8 Select the text or paragraphs and open the Borders and Shading dialogue box.

9 Click None in the Settings area.

You can apply Shading to selected text or whole paragraphs, using the Shading tool and the tab in the Borders and Shading dialogue box.

To add shading

10 Select the text or paragraph(s) you want to add shading to.

11 For a solid colour, click the down arrow by the Shading tool and pick from the palette.

or

12 If you want a patterned shade, open the Borders and Shading dialogue box and switch to the Shading tab.

13 Select the Fill (background) colour.

14 Set the pattern style.

15 Select the second colour.

16 Click OK.

Important

You can apply borders to selected sides, by clicking on them in the Borders and Shading drop-down list, but note that clicking the Borders and Shading tool directly selects whichever option you last used. Use it to open the dialogue box for greatest flexibility.

Applying a page border

If you are producing a poster, brochure, certificate or similar document, you might want to add a border around the whole page. This is easily done.

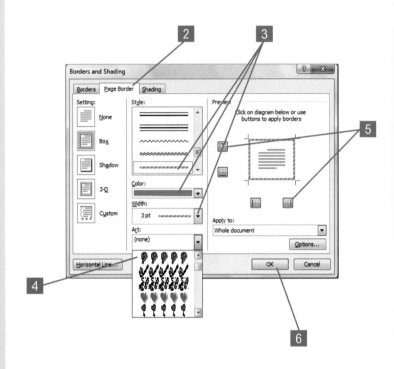

1. Click the arrow on the Borders and Shading tool and select the Borders and Shading dialogue box.

2. Switch to the Page Border tab.

3. Define the Style, Colour and Width of the line, as for other borders.

   or

4. Select a decorative border from the Art drop down list.

5. If you do not want the border on certain sides, click on their icons in the Preview area.

6. Click OK.

If you need to lay out data in neat columns and rows, the simplest way to do this is with a table.

If you want to create a simple regular table, click the Table button on the Insert tab. Whatever size you set at the start is not fixed – rows and columns can be added or deleted later.

You can either create the table by setting the size on a grid, or by using the Insert Table dialogue box. The second approach lets you choose the AutoFit behaviour which sets how the table fits around its contents and within the window.

1 Place the cursor where the table is to go.

2 Switch to the Insert tab on the Ribbon and click the Table button.

3 Drag across the grid to set the size.

   or

4 Select the Insert Table command.

5 At the Insert Table dialogue box, set the number of rows and columns.

6 Choose the AutoFit behaviour which will work best in the document.

7 Click OK

▶

Creating a table (cont.)

8 The Table Design tools will be at the front of the Ribbon. Select a Table style.

9 Enter data into the cells, formatting the text if required. Press the Tab key to move from one cell to the next, or click into a cell with the mouse.

Timesaver tip

You can change the table style at any point, without losing any of the data that you have entered, or any of the formatting that you have applied to text.

Text within cells can be formatted as normal – once it has been selected.

To select:

- A word: double-click in it.

- All the text in one cell: triple-click in it.

- A column: hover the mouse over the top border. When the cursor becomes a thick arrow, click to select the column.

- A row: double-click by the left border.

- Any block of cells: drag the mouse over them.

There are extra alignment options in cells. The contents can be aligned vertically as well as horizontally, and text can also be written up or down – very handy for headings or narrow columns of figures.

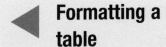
To set the alignment

1 Bring the Table Layout tab to the front of the Ribbon.

2 Select the cell, row or column to be formatted.

3 Click on an alignment option.

or

4 Click the Text Direction tool. The text will be written downwards. Click again to write it upwards, or again to go back to normal.

Timesaver tip

When you change the text direction, the row will be made much deeper. If you decide not to use a vertical option, it will not shrink back by itself. Use the Row height field to reduce it.

Modifying a table

A table's size, shape and layout can be changed at any time – even after data has been entered into it. You can:

- Insert or delete rows or columns.
- Change the width of columns.
- Change the overall size of the table.

To insert a row or column

1 Click into a cell in the row or column adjacent to where the new one will go.

2 Right-click, point to Insert and select an option.

To delete rows or columns

3 Click into a cell in the row or column, or drag across (or down) the table to select two or more rows or columns.

4 Right-click and select the Delete option on the context menu.

To change the column width

5 Point to the dividing line on the right of a column to get the double-headed arrow, then drag the line left or right to set the width.

or

6 Drag on the column marker on the ruler.

To change the table size

7 Point to a corner so the cursor becomes the resize arrow, then drag the table outline to the required size.

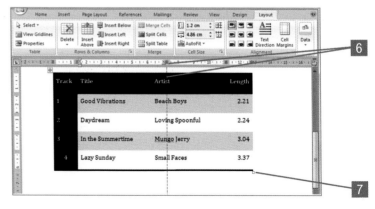

Some characters cannot be typed directly from the keyboard, but that doesn't mean that you cannot use them in your documents. You just have to get them from another source. The Insert Symbol routine lets you access the untypeable!

1 Place the insertion point where you want the character to go.

2 On the Insert tab, click on the Symbol button.

3 Select a commonly-used symbol from the display.

or

4 Click More Symbols to open the Symbol dialogue box.

5 Pick a font from the list – you will find the biggest choice of symbols and graphics in the Symbol, Wingding and Webding fonts.

6 Click on a character to see an enlargement.

7 Click Insert to insert the selected character into your text.

8 Click ⊠ to close the Symbol dialogue box.

? Did you know?

There is a collection of special characters on the other tab in the Symbol dialogue box. These are mainly used in professional typesetting.

Inserting pictures

Word can handle graphics files in many formats including BMP, JPG, GIF, Photo CD and possibly many more, depending upon which graphic converter routines have been installed. The pictures may have been captured by a scanner or digital camera, downloaded from the web, or drawn in a graphics program.

1 Place the pointer where you want to insert the picture.

2 On the Insert tab, click Picture in the Illustrations group.

3 The Insert Picture dialogue box will open. Go to the folder holding the file.

4 Select the file.

5 Click Insert.

The only real difference between clip art and other pictures is where it comes from. Clip art comes from clip art collections. A small collection is supplied with Microsoft Office, but a much larger one is available at Office Online. You may be asked if you want to include the online collection in the search, though that option may already be turned on. This gives you lots more choice, but takes longer.

1 Open the Insert tab and click Clip Art – the Clip Art task pane will open.

2 Type the Search for word(s).

3 Drop down the Results should be menu. List and tick the types of media that you want.

4 Click Go.

5 Scroll through the results to find a picture.

6 To insert the image, double-click or click the arrow bar and select Insert.

7 Close the Task pane if no longer required.

Timesaver tip

You can preview sounds, video clips, animated GIFs and similar files in the Clip Art Task pane.

Formatting pictures

After inserting a picture or clip art, you can adjust its size and position, change its brightness, the contrast or the shades of colour, and add a border or other effects. The tools are on the Format tab on the Ribbon. This should come to the front automatically when a picture is selected.

You can adjust the colours and tones in different ways – and very easily. The Brightness and Contrast tools are in the Adjust group and are used in the same way.

To change the size or position

1 To adjust the size, click on a handle and drag in or out.

2 To keep it in proportion, hold down Shift and drag on a corner handle.

3 To centre the image, select it, then go to the Home tab and click the Centre tool in the Alignment group.

or

4 Click the Position tool and select a Text Wrapping option – this controls how the image fits with the text.

To adjust the colours

5 Click the Brightness or Contrast button to drop down the options – you can adjust the levels up or down by 40%.

6 Point to a setting – Live Preview will show you how it will look.

7 Click on the setting to apply it.

If you want to create new images, pick out points on imported pictures, or add arrows, blobs or blocks of background colour, there is a handy set of tools on the Drawing toolbar.

In a drawn picture, each item remains separate and can be moved, resized, recoloured or deleted at any later time. (Though items can be joined into Groups or placed inside picture frames, for convenient handling.) This is quite different from Paint and similar packages, where each addition becomes merged permanently into the whole picture.

1. Click into the document where you want to draw the picture.

7

2. On the Insert tab of the Ribbon, click Shapes and select New Drawing Canvas from the bottom of the menu.

3. A blank frame will appear, and the Drawing Format tools tab will come to the front of the Ribbon.

4. Select a line or shape tool from the Insert Shapes set.

5. Click and drag to draw the shape.

6. Click and drag on the corner and edge handles to adjust the shape.

7. Drag the green handle if you want to rotate the shape.

8. Use the Shape Styles options to set the outline and fill colour, and fill shading style,

and/or

9. Use the Fill and Outline tools to colour the object.

10. Click the More button on the Insert Shapes set to see the full range of tools.

Drawing pictures (cont.)

10

11. To add a shadow, select the object then click the Shadow Effects tool and pick a style.

12. If a 3D effect is required, click the 3-D Effect button. Select the perspective and rotation, then adjust the appearance with the Depth, Direction, Lighting and Surface options.

11

12

Drawing pictures (cont.)

13 The drawing canvas can sit in line with text, i.e. in a space between paragraphs, or text can be wrapped round it in several ways. To change this, click on the background of the canvas to select the whole thing, then click the Position tool and choose an option. Live Preview will show you the effect if you hover the mouse over an option.

14 If you want objects to line up with each other or to be equally spaced, select them then click the Align button and select an option.

15 Click outside the canvas area when you want to return to normal text editing.

Using columns

Word's layout facilities are almost as good as you will find in dedicated DTP (desktop publishing) software – its handling of columns is a good example.

You can set text in two or three columns, of the same or different widths, over the whole document or a selected part.

1. Select the text to set if only part is to be in columns.

2. On the Page Layout tab, click the Columns button.

3. For equally spaced columns, or for a standard wide + narrow combination, click the option.

   or

4. To define the layout yourself, click More Columns.

5. Select the closest Preset design to set the number of columns.

6. Clear Equal column width and adjust the Width or Spacing if required.

7. Tick the Line between checkbox if a line is required.

8. Set the Apply to option.

9. Click OK.

In a mail merge, a standard letter is combined with names and addresses from a data file to produce personalised letters or mailing labels. The data file can come from Access or another database system, or be created within Word. Its data is drawn into the Word document through merge fields, which link to fields in the data file.

Setting up a mail merge is straightforward, and is made even easier by the Mail Merge Wizard, which guides you through the process.

There are three stages:

- Create the main document – typically a standard letter or circular.
- Create the data source – which may mean typing the data into a new file, or locating an existing file.
- Merge the data into the document. There are three aspects to this:
  1. Inserting the merge fields into the document.
  2. Selecting the records to include from the data file.
  3. Outputting the merged letters.

The main document

This will have all its text, apart from the name and address, and perhaps other details of its recipients. It will be formatted and have its page setup and other options set, so that it is ready to run once the data has been added.

7

Important

The Address List is a simple database. If you want to reuse it later, it can be edited through the Mail Merge routine before running a merge.

Running a mail merge (cont.)

Creating the main document

1. When the document is ready, save it then switch to the Mailings tab, click the Start Mail Merge button and select Mail Merge Wizard.

2. Select the document type and click Next.

3. Select the starting document – in this example, I am using the current document – then click Next.

4. If you were using an existing data file, it would be opened now. Your contacts list in Outlook or the Address Book, which holds the email addresses and other details of your contacts, could also be used.

5 If you choose Type a new list, the New Address List dialogue box will open. Enter the address information for the recipients, clicking New Entry after each.

6 Click Close when you are done. You will be taken to the Save As dialogue box. Give a file name and select a folder to hold the file.

7 You will be shown the recipient list. Check it, and if necessary click the Edit button to go back in to it to edit entries or add more. Click OK.

8 When you get back to the Wizard, click Next: Write your letter to move to the next step.

Running a mail merge (cont.)

If the letter has not yet been written, or it needs editing, the text can be typed now. This is also the time for bringing in information from the data source.

Incorporating data

9 Place the insertion point where you want the first field to be written.

10 Select the Address block, Greeting line or other item from the list in the Task pane.

11 A dialogue box will open. Set the options for the item as required and click OK.

12 Click Next to preview your letters.

7

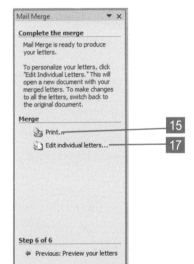

13 At the preview stage, check through enough of your letters to see how the merge will work. If the text or fields need to be edited, do that now.

14 Click Next to complete the merge.

15 If no further editing is required, click Print.

16 Select the records to print and click OK.

17 If you want to personalise the mailing, click Edit individual letters and edit selected merged letters as required before printing.

Digital photography

Introduction

Digital cameras have transformed photography over the last decade or so, and have changed the way that we use computers. Storing, viewing, editing and printing digital photos have become, for many people, their main computing activity. Now we all have our 'darkrooms' where we can crop, frame, recolour and enhance our captured images. The PC is also the filing cabinet, the display album and the printshop.

Digital cameras always come with their own software for organising and editing photos. I would recommend ignoring it, and I am not covering it in this book. You are generally better off using Windows Explorer to handle your image files – the camera software tends to be more complicated in its file storage. And the editing routines in Windows Live Photo Gallery are sophisticated, but normally simpler to use than those in most camera software suites. There's another advantage to staying with the Windows software for your digital photography work – if you change your camera, you will not need to learn how to use a new set of programs.

What you'll do

Store digital photos

Use Photo Gallery

Undo editing

Adjust exposure

Adjust colour

Straighten a photo

Crop a photo

Use black and white effects

File from Photo Gallery

Print photos

Burn a disk from Photo Gallery

Storing digital photos

It is so simple to copy or move photos from your digital camera onto your Windows PC. Windows treats the memory card in the camera as if it were a removable hard drive or CD – all you need to do is connect them together. You can do this in two ways: either use a cable to link a USB port on the PC with the USB port on your camera, or take the memory card out of the camera and plug it directly into the matching card slot on your PC. (Not all PCs have these.)

To use Windows import

We'll use the USB connection. There are four different ways that you can transfer the files onto your PC through the USB link:

1. Link the camera and the PC with a USB cable, and turn the camera on. You may need to switch it to display mode.

- Using Windows Import routine. This creates a folder, labelled with the date and – optionally – a tag, copies the images into it and adds the tag to the names of the image files.

2. The first time that you do this – and until you set the default – the AutoPlay window will ask you how you want to handle the device.

- Using Windows Live Photo gallery. This gives you more control, allowing you to select which images to import and, bringing in the images in smaller groups, each of which can be tagged separately.

3. Select Import Pictures and Videos using Windows.

- Using Windows Explorer. This treats the camera's memory just as if it were a disk drive, and files can be transferred from – or to – the camera by the usual drag and drop techniques. If you put the memory card into a card reader, this is the only option you have.

- If you installed the software which came with the camera, then this will have an import routine. I have yet to meet one that is better, simpler or more efficient than any of the three Windows alternatives, so I shall ignore this.

4 If you enter a tag at this stage it will be added to the folder name, and to the name of each of the images.

5 Click Import.

6 At the Importing dialogue box, tick the Erase after importing checkbox if you want to clear the camera's memory.

7 The new folder will be in your Pictures folder, and the images will have been numbered.

8

Timesaver tip

When you have decided which import technique you prefer, next time you use it, tick the Always do this for this device at the AutoPlay dialogue box.

Digital photography 199

Storing digital photos (cont.)

To use Windows Explorer

1. Link the camera and the PC with a USB cable, and turn the camera on.

2. At the AutoPlay window select Open device to view files using Windows Explorer.

3. A new Explorer window will open, showing the top level folder on the camera's memory. Open the folders down to the one holding the photos.

4. If you want to create a new folder (e.g. within your Pictures folder) in which to store the files, do so now.

5. You must be able to see the folder that you want to store the pictures in and the one on the camera. Adjust the Navigation display to bring the target folder into view, or open a new Explorer window and open the target folder in that.

6. Select the photos you want to transfer to your PC.

Storing digital photos (cont.)

To copy photos, leaving them in the camera memory

7 Drag the selected photos across and drop them in the target folder.

or

To move photos from the camera memory onto your PC

8 Hold down the right mouse button as you drag the photos. When you drop them into the target folder, a menu will appear – select Move Here.

9 Wait while the photos are transferred.

Important

If your PC has a suitable card reader slot, and you put your camera's memory into it, an Explorer window will open automatically.

8

Storing digital photos (cont.)

To import using the Gallery

1. Link the camera and the PC with a USB cable, and turn the camera on.

2. At the AutoPlay window select Import Pictures and Videos using Windows Live Photo Gallery.

3. If you want all the images, select Import all new items now. The routine is almost the same as Import using Windows Explorer – follow from steps 4 on page 199.

   otherwise

4. Select Review, organise and group items to import and click Next.

5. The photos will be grouped according to when they were taken. You can change the time span – and therefore the size of the groups – by dragging the Adjust groups slider.

6. Enter a name for any groups that you want to import.

7. If you do not want all the items in a group, click the View all … items link, then clear the ticks from the unwanted images.

Storing digital photos (cont.)

8 When you have worked through all the groups, click Import.

9 At the Importing dialogue box, tick the Erase after importing checkbox if you want to clear the camera's memory.

10 A new folder will have been created for every group in your Pictures folder. They will have the names you gave to the groups, or names based on the date.

Using Photo Gallery

Windows Live Photo Gallery is one of the programs available for free download from the Windows Live site. If you haven't already got them, download them now. (See page 73.). It may be called 'gallery' but this is far more than just a viewer for your photos. You can use it to copy, delete, print, email, or edit any picture file.

Once you have opened the gallery for one file, you can use it to work through the other images in the same folder.

1. In Windows Explorer, open the folder that contains the pictures you want to view or edit.

2. Select a photo.

3. Click the Down arrow by the Open button on the toolbar.

4. Select Windows Live Photo Gallery.

   or

5. Right-click on the photo, point to Open With and select Windows Live Photo Gallery.

6. When the Photo Gallery opens, explore its tools.

204

Previous   Next   Rotate Left   Slide show   Actual size/   Zoom
                                                  fit to window   slider
                              Delete

                    Rotate Right

8

Digital photography 205

Undoing editing

Like all good editing software, Photo Gallery has an Undo facility, which means that you can try out ideas without ruining your photo.

Undo will undo the changes made during an editing session. When you return to the Gallery, any edits will be saved – however, if you bring the photo back into Fix mode, the Undo button will then offer you a Revert option, allowing you to get back to the original picture.

Undo all the changes made in this and previous editing sessions

Click to undo the last action

Click the arrow to open the list and select the earliest action to undo – all those above will also be undone.

The beauty of digital photography is that, unlike film-based photography, the picture you see is not the final image. You can adjust and improve the picture in a variety of ways – and you don't need a darkroom to change the exposure or the colour balance.

1 Click Fix on the toolbar above the picture.

2 Click Adjust Exposure in the sidebar on the right. A small panel will open below.

3 Drag the Brightness and Colour sliders to adjust the levels.

4 Use the Shadows and Highlights sliders to fine-tune the contrast levels.

5 If you do not like the changes you have made, click Undo to go back.

6 If you have moved on to another picture, and then returned to an adjusted one, you can still undo the changes, but you will be asked if you want to revert to the original version. Click Revert to do so.

8

Digital photography 207

Adjusting the colour

In digital photographs, as in any kind of computer images, colours are produced by mixing red, blue and green light. By varying the combinations and intensity, the full range of hues and shades can be generated. Photo Gallery gives you three ways to adjust colours:

- Colour temperature controls the amount of blue in the image – a high level of blue makes it look cold!

- Tint controls the green red balance.

- Saturation controls the overall amount of colour, on a scale which goes from pure greys to very vibrant colours.

1 If the editing sidebar is not already open, click Fix.

2 Click Adjust Colour to open its panel.

3 Drag Colour Temperature to the left to increase the level of blue.

4 Drag the Tint slider to the left to increase the green level, or right for a redder image.

5 Drag the Saturation slider to the left to make the picture greyer, or to the right for richer colours.

Timesaver tip

Nudge all the sliders to the right to give outdoor shots a sun-drenched feel.

208

If your horizon isn't horizontal, or your subjects are leaning when you'd like them to be upright, the Straighten feature can sort it out. This allows you to rotate the photo by up to about 10° in either direction. As it is rotated, the photo is slightly enlarged so that it still fills the original rectangle.

Straightening a photo

If the editing sidebar is not open, click Fix.

Click Straighten Photo to open its panel.

Using the grid of vertical and horizontal lines as a guide, drag the slider to rotate the photo.

When you are happy with the result, click Straighten Photo again to close the panel.

8

Cropping a picture

It often seems to be more difficult to frame a photo accurately with a digital camera than with a traditional one. The screens can be hard to see on sunny days, and the viewfinders – if present – are rarely good guides. But it's not a major problem because you can easily crop a photo to remove unwanted material from around the central image.

Cropping is also useful before printing a picture. If you ensure that the image has the same proportions as the paper, then – though it may be shrunk or expanded to fit – it will not be distorted in the printed image.

1 If the editing sidebar is not already open, click Fix.

2 Click Crop Photo to open the cropping panel.

3 Open the Proportion drop-down list.

4 Select the size that you want to use for printing, or otherwise outputting the image.

5 Click Rotate Frame if you need to switch from landscape to portrait layout, or vice versa.

6 A bright rectangle indicates the area to be retained after cropping. Drag the corners of the outline to change the cropped size.

7 Click anywhere within the rectangle and drag to move the crop area.

8 When you are happy with the selection, click Apply.

Digital photos are always captured in colour, but some images can look better, or more interesting, or more striking, in black and white, or sepia. You can convert an image to monochrome using the Black and white effects options.

1 If the editing sidebar is not open, click Fix.

2 Click Black and white effects to see the set of options.

3 Click on an effect to apply it to the photo.

4 If you do not like any of the effects, use Undo to restore the coloured image.

5 Click Black and white effects again to close the options panel.

6 Open the Adjust exposure panel and tweak the brightness and contrast.

Digital photography 211

Filing from Photo Gallery

You can use Photo Gallery to perform the usual filing jobs, like deleting, copying and renaming, but you can also do more. For a start, there are two copying operations.

The Copy command copies the image to the Windows Clipboard so that it can be pasted into another application.

Make a copy copies the file either into another folder and/or with a different name. It will still be the same type – if you want to save the file as a different type, you need to open it in Paint or another graphics program.

There is also a Revert to Original option here, which can be very handy if your adjusting and cropping efforts have not gone as well as you had hoped.

To copy a file

1. Click the File button to open its menu.

2. To copy to the Clipboard, so that you can paste it elsewhere, select Copy.

   or

3. Select Make a Copy... to open the Make a Copy dialogue box.

4. If you want to keep the copy in the same folder (or if you just want to change the name anyway), edit the File name.

5. If you want to save it in a different folder, type the path, or select it from the drop-down list at the top, or click Browse folders and select the folder there.

6. Click Save.

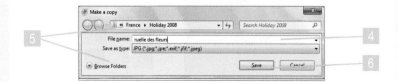

Photo Gallery has a print routine that will print one or more photos at a time, on a range of paper sizes, with a variety of layouts. If you want to print more than one photo – as distinct from several copies of the same photo – you must first switch to the Gallery's alternative display, where you can select multiple pictures.

To print a single photo

Click the Print button on the toolbar and select Print.

To print several photos at once

Make sure your printer is loaded with the right type of paper.

Click the Go To Gallery button on the toolbar.

In the Explorer-style display, select the photos you want to print.

Click the Print button and select Print...

Printing photos (cont.)

6   At the Print Pictures window, select the Printer, Paper size, Quality and Paper type.

7   Pick a layout from the list on the right.

8   If you want more than one copy of each picture, set the number.

9   Click Print.

You might want to copy photos (or other files) onto a recordable CD or DVD:

- To give to a friend.

- To take to the camera shop for printing – it typically costs about half as much to have them printed in a shop than to print them yourself, and you will usually get a better quality result.

- As backup, in case your PC goes wrong – it happens! If you value your photos, keep copies on disks.

This is much the same as burning a disk through Explorer (see page 158) which is not surprising, as the Gallery uses the same routines! The main difference is that you start by selecting the photos you want to copy. You do not have to add them all at once. You can select one set, burn them, then select and burn some more, until you have all the ones you want, or you run out of space.

Burning a disk from Photo Gallery

1. Use the tags or other ways of sorting the photos to find the ones you want.

2. Select the photos.

3. If there is no CD/DVD in the drive, put one in now.

4. Click the Make button and select Burn a DVD or Burn a data CD…

5. Give the disk a title, wait while it is formatted (if necessary) and the files are copied over.

6. Add more photos, if you like, then when you have done, press the button on the drive to eject the disk. Windows will make sure the files are safely stored before ejecting it.

8

More about Windows

9

Introduction

In this chapter we will go a little deeper into Windows. None of this is essential for the day-to-day running of your PC, and I know of quite a few long-time PC users who have never got round to exploring any of the features covered here – and never missed it. I think they are missing out. The more you understand about the possibilities of your PC, the more you can do, and the easier you can do things. Most of the things dealt with in this chapter are ways to adapt the Windows environment so that it is easier for you to work with. Read on and find out how to change the appearance of the screen – perhaps to make it more accessible, or simply to make it look the way you like it; tailor the mouse to your touch; organise the Start menu, Task bar and the Desktop; set up the PC for multiple users; and add gadgets to your Desktop.

Exploring the Control Panel

The Control Panel lets you customise some aspects of Windows to your own tastes.

Some settings are best left at the defaults; some should be set when new hardware or software is added to the system; some should be set once then left alone; a few can be adjusted at any time.

What is in your Control panel depends upon the hardware and software on your system. Open yours to see what is there.

1 Click the Start button.

2 Select Control Panel.

3 The Control Panel has two alternative display modes. The default view groups the controls according to what they do. This is probably the best for new users. Click on a link to see the next level.

4 At the second level of the Control Panel, you can pick a task or an icon to adjust a setting.

5 Click the Back button to return to the top level.

6 The Control Panel can also be viewed using an icons display. In this mode you have direct access to the controls – but you need to know what you are looking for. Click the View by button on the top right and select Large or Small icons.

7 If you want to switch back to the default view, click the View by button and select Category.

9

Setting the Date and Time

The date and time can be adjusted if you want, though this should rarely be necessary. You can get Windows to handle Summer Time changes for you, and even get it to keep the clock accurate automatically.

1 In the Control Panel click the Clock, Language and Region link.

2 Select Date and Time.

3 On the Date & Time tab, click Change Date and Time.

4 Use the Calendar to set the date.

5 Select the hour and minute figures in turn and type in the correct value.

6 Click on OK.

7 Click Change Time Zone and use the drop-down list if it needs changing.

8 Click OK to close and save your changes.

Did you know?

You can have several clocks if you need to know the time in different time zones. Set them up on the Additional Clocks tab.

Timesaver tip

On the Internet Time tab you can turn on an option to synchronise the clock with an Internet time server. It will then check the time once a week automatically. If you are online regularly, this is well worth doing.

Windows display options are not just decorative. If you spend a lot of time in front of your screen, it is important that you can see it clearly and use it comfortably.

A theme sets the overall style for the Desktop – its background image, the icons for the standard Windows tools, the colours and fonts, and the sounds that are triggered by alerts and prompts. If there are parts of the theme that you don't like, you can modify them on the other tabs. If you are used to earlier versions of Windows you can switch to the Classic display.

Themes have an impact on every part of the display.

Customising the display

Selecting a theme

1. Start from Appearance and Personalisation and select Change the theme.

2. Scroll through the list and click on a theme. Its first image will be applied to the Desktop, and its startup sound played.

3. If you don't like them, try another.

Timesaver tip

If you modify a theme, click Save As and save it with a new name. If you ever change the theme, you can then easily restore your carefully modified one.

9

Customising the display (cont.)

Choosing a Wallpaper

1. At the Control Panel, select Appearance and Personalisation, then Change desktop background.

2. Select a Picture Location from the drop-down list – Windows Desktop Backgrounds has a good set of suitable images.

    or

3. Click Browse and find the folder that contains the image you want to use.

4. Select one or more images – when you point to a thumbnail, a checkbox will appear at the top left. Click to select or deselect the image.

5. Choose how you want the picture to be positioned – if it is not big enough to fill the screen, it can be stretched to fit, or tiled as a pattern.

6. Set the Change picture every … time – anything from 10 seconds to 1 day.

7. Click Save changes to apply the choice.

8. Click the Back button to return to the Personalisation options.

▶

The Desktop

The Wallpaper is the background to the Desktop. There is a set of designs to choose from, or you can use any image (in .BMP, .GIF or .JPG format) or a web page.

Many themes have a changing background, with a set of images that switch round every 30 minutes. You can add more images, change the display time, or have a single, fixed image.

See also

There's more about tidying the Desktop on page 239.

The colour selection that you make here will be applied to the windows, the Task bar and the Start menu. You can choose from preset colours, or mix your own.

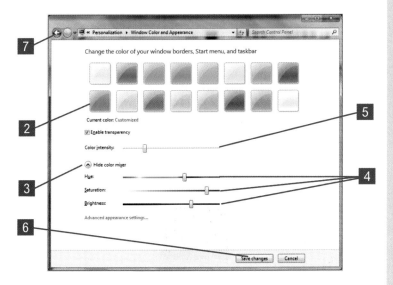

Using colours

1 At the Control Panel, select Appearance and Personalisation, then Change window glass colours.

2 Pick a colour.

or

3 Click Show colour mixer (its label will then change to Hide colour mixer).

4 Use the sliders to set the hue, saturation and brightness.

5 Set the Colour intensity level – move the slider to the left to increase transparency.

6 Click OK to apply the choice.

7 Click the Back button to return to the Personalisation options.

9

Customising the display (cont.)

Setting a screen saver

1. At the Control Panel select Appearance and Personalisation, then Change screen saver.

2. Select a screen saver from the drop-down list and click Preview to run it on screen.

3. Click Settings and set the options to suit yourself.

4. For password protection, turn on the option On resume, display logon screen.

5. Click Apply to apply your choices but keep the dialogue box open.

A screen saver switches to a moving image after the system has been inactive for a few minutes. These were useful on old monitors, as static images could burn into the screen if left on too long. This is not a problem with new monitors, but screen savers still have their uses. If you set it to be password protected, once the screen saver has started, it can only be turned off by entering the password – so you can leave your desk knowing that your work will be safe from passers-by once the screen saver starts up.

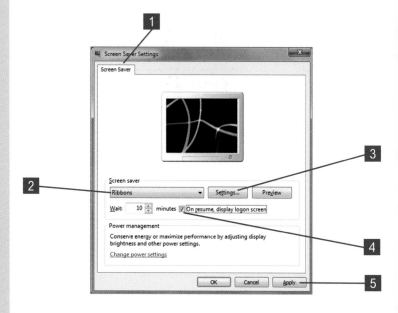

▶

224

The Photos option in the screen savers gives you a constantly changing display of images. It's ideal for running a slide show of your favourite photos. These can be collected into a single folder, or marked by a special tag.

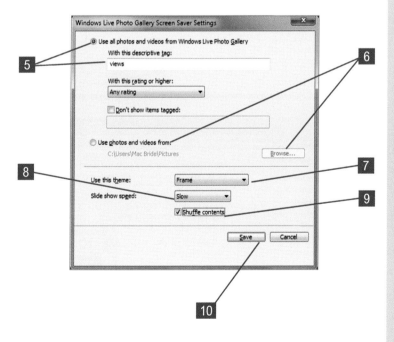

Slide show screen savers

1 Locate your favourite photos or other images and move or copy them into one folder.

2 Go to the Screen saver routine in the Control Panel.

3 Select Photos as the screen saver.

4 Click Settings to open the Photo Screen Saver Settings dialogue box.

5 Select Use all pictures from the Photo Gallery, and specify the selection with a tag.

or

6 Click Use pictures and videos from and set the folder to use.

7 Specify the theme – this sets the style of the display and of the transitions between slides.

8 Set the speed.

9 Turn on Shuffle contents to randomise the order.

10 Click Save to save the settings and return to the screen saver tab.

9

Defining the
screen settings

▶

The Display settings control the resolution and colours of the monitor screen. Finding the right resolution for you is a matter of the balance between quality and quantity – more pixels give you larger windows but smaller type. Higher Colours settings produce a prettier screen but take more memory and time to update. Find the levels that you can work best with.

Do not change the Advanced options unless the current display is not working properly *and* you know what you are doing. You can switch to a display mode that is not properly supported by your hardware, resulting in a screen which is impossible to read – and therefore impossible to correct!

1 On the Control Panel select Display, then Adjust screen resolution.

2 Adjust the Resolution – try it at the highest setting first. If you do not like this, try the next one down until you reach the right level for you.

3 If the screen text is hard to read, click Make text and other items larger or smaller.

4 Select the Medium option and click Apply.

5 Click OK – the new settings will be applied.

6 A dialogue box will appear asking if you want to keep the new settings. Click Revert at the prompt to go back to the original ones.

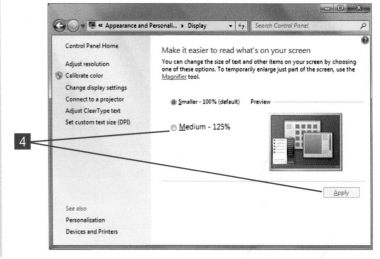

Work in Windows is much easier if you are comfortable with your mouse. Use the Mouse Properties panel to set the way that it responds.

Don't change to Left-handed unless you are the only one who uses the PC, and it is the only system that you ever use. Ideally, you should learn to use the mouse with either hand.

- The Double-Click Speed sets the difference between a double-click and two separate clicks.
- Pointer Speed links speed and distance, so that the faster you move the mouse, the further the pointer goes.

Find speeds that suit you and stick with them. If you keep changing them, you will never get the feel of the mouse.

1. Open the Control Panel. Under Hardware and Sound, select Mouse.

2. On the Buttons panel, set the Double-click speed and double-click in the Test area to see if the system responds.

3. Click Apply.

4. Go to the Pointer Options panel.

5. Set the Pointer Speed.

6. Click Apply to test the new speed setting.

7. Turn on the Pointer trails and set the size.

8. Click OK to close and keep your settings.

9

Did you know?

A pointer trail makes the mouse easier to see on LCD screens.

Attaching sounds to events

Windows allows you to attach sounds to events. These can be seen as useful ways of alerting you to what's happening or as more modern noise pollution. It all depends upon your point of view. I like a fanfare when the system is ready to start work (to wake me up – well, you wait so long!) but few other sounds. Try them out – the Utopia sounds are worth listening to.

The other tabs can be used to change the Audio and Voice devices or fine-tune their volume controls. The devices are best left to the system. The volume controls can be reached more simply from the icon on the Taskbar.

1 At the Control Panel select Hardware and Sound, then Change system sounds.

2 Open the Sounds tab.

3 Pick a Scheme.

4 Select an event.

5 Click Test to preview its sound.

6 Sample a few more and go back to Step 3 and try alternative schemes until you find one you prefer.

7 To set individual sounds, select the event then pick a new sound from the Sounds list or Browse for an alternative.

8 Click Apply or OK.

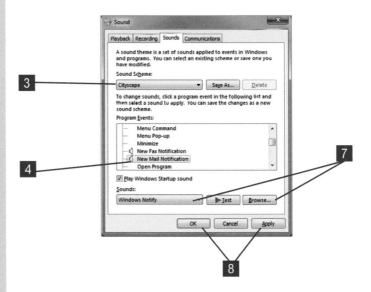

Important

You can use the Test hardware and Troubleshoot routines on the Audio, Voice and Hardware tabs if you have problems with the sound systems.

The volume can be controlled in several ways. The simplest, of course, is to use the knob on your speakers, or if you are too lazy to reach across the desk, you can use the volume control on the Task bar.

You can also set the volume separately for each application that produces sound, e.g. you could set the system sounds that alert you to errors, incoming mail and the like, to a lower level so that they don't interrupt the CD that you are listening to.

You can also configure the system to match your speaker setup.

Controlling the volume

1 Click the Volume Control icon 🔊 on the right of the Task bar.

2 Drag the slider up or down as required.

or

3 Click the Mute icon 🔊 to turn the sounds off completely (or back on again).

To adjust the volume mix

4 On the volume control, click Mixer.

5 Set the overall volume for the device.

6 Set the level for each application that you have running.

To set up your speakers

7 Right-click on the Volume Control icon and select Playback Devices.

8 At the Sounds dialogue box, select the device and click Configure.

9 Choose your configuration, and click Test to check it.

10 Click Next to customise the setup, then Finish.

9

Setting Regional options

The Region and Language options control the units of measurement and the styles used by applications for displaying dates, time, currency and other numbers. The choice of region sets the basic formats, but any or all of these can be customised.

1. Start from Clock, Language and Region in the Control Panel and click Region and Language.

2. On the Formats tab select the country.

3. To change a date or time option, click on the bar and choose from the drop-down list.

To customise the settings

4. Click the Additional settings button.

5. Work through the tabs.

6. To change any aspect, pick from its drop-down list.

7. Click OK.

Timesaver tip

The Date and Time can be set more easily through the Clock – see page 220.

The Keyboards and Languages tab lets you enter foreign language text using the keyboard. This changes the letters produced by the keys and is best suited to touch-typists who are used to a foreign keyboard. Most of us are better off selecting foreign characters from the Character Map.

Adding other languages

1 In the Region and Language dialogue box, switch to the Keyboards and Languages tab.

2 Click Change keyboards.

3 At the Text Services and Input Languages box, click Add and then pick the language.

4 To define a shortcut for switching the keyboard, use the Advanced Key Settings tab.

5 Click OK.

9

For your information

If you have other languages installed on your PC and want to use them in your dialogue boxes and menus, click the Install/uninstall languages… button and follow the instructions. If you would like to install other languages, go to the Microsoft website and search for 'Language Interface Pack'. There are lots available for free download.

Improving accessibility

Windows offers a range of ways to make life easier for people with sight, hearing or motor control disabilities – though the keyboard alternative to the mouse may well be useful to other people as well.

Using the Keyboard

1 On the Control Panel, select Ease of Access, and then click Change how your keyboard works.

2 Turn on Mouse Keys to use the number pad as a control for the mouse pointer.

3 Turn on Sticky Keys if you want to be able to type Ctrl, Shift and Alt combinations by pressing one key at a time, rather than all at once.

4 Turn on Toggle Keys if you want to be alerted by a sound when any of the Lock keys are pressed.

5 Turn on Filter Keys if you find that keystrokes are sometimes repeated because you type very slowly.

6 Click the Set up link in any of these areas to fine tune the settings.

7 Click Save.

Important

You can replace the sounds that Windows uses to alert you to events with visible alerts, using the options on the Sound tab of this dialogue box.

You can also make the mouse easier to see, or replace it with keystrokes. If the Mouse Keys option is turned on, the arrow keys on the Number pad can be used to move the mouse pointer, and the central key (5) acts as the left mouse button. Movement is more limited than an actual mouse – you can only move up, down, left or right and not diagonally – but it is easier to control.

Setting up Mouse Keys

1 At the Ease of Access Centre, select Change how your mouse works.

2 Set the size and colour of the mouse pointer.

3 Tick the checkbox to turn on Mouse Keys.

4 Click the Set up Mouse Keys link to adjust the key settings.

5 Experiment with the Speed and Acceleration settings to find the most workable levels.

6 If you click Apply, the settings will be activated without you leaving this window.

7 When you are happy with the settings, click OK.

8 Click the Back button to return to the Ease of Access Centre.

9

More about Windows 233

Improving accessibility (cont.)

To use a high contrast display

1 In the Ease of Access Centre, select Optimise visual display.

2 Click Choose a High Contrast colour scheme.

3 At the Change the visuals window, scroll through the themes and select a high contrast one. It will be applied immediately.

4 Close the window.

5 If you want to be able to switch between high contrast and normal, tick the Turn on or off High Contrast checkbox, then set its options.

6 For audio assistance, turn on the Narrator and/or Audio Description options.

To improve visibility

7 Click Change the size of text and icons. At the Scaling dialogue box, set the new scale and click OK.

8 Turn on the Magnifier.

9 Making the cursor thicker and setting a slower blink rate can make it easier to see.

10 Click OK when you have finished.

Optimising the display

There are several ways to make the screen easier to read. A high contrast colour scheme is the most obvious of these. Others include the Narrator, which will read any text on the screen, the Magnifier which zooms in on the area under the cursor, and changing the size and blink rate of the cursor.

The Start menu can be customised in several ways. You can very easily change its appearance and control which items are shown in the main display. With just a little more effort, you can also reorganise shortcuts in the All Programs area, adding, moving or removing them as required.

The Start menu will normally list the programs you have used recently, and the documents that you opened with them. This is convenient, but can be turned off if you don't want other people to see what you have been working on.

You saw earlier that there are several ways to end a session, and that you select these from the menu that opens off the power button on the Start menu. You can set, as the default, whichever option you use most often, so that this is selected when you click the button.

1 Right-click on the Start button and select Properties.

2 Select the action to be run from the power button.

3 Clear the checkboxes for Store and display... if you don't want other people to know what you are working on.

4 Click OK.

! Important

If you are one of several users on a PC, remember that every user has his or her own Start menu, so feel free to customise yours to suit yourself.

9

Customising the Start menu (cont.)

The standard items, such as Computer, Documents and Games can be displayed as a menu, a link to a window – or not at all. The system notes which programs you use most often, and includes these in the Start menu. You can set how many to include.

The Start menu

1 Open the Start menu properties dialogue box.

2 Work through the main list of options, setting how – or if – you want standard items to be displayed.

3 Set the number of recent programs to show on the menu.

4 Click OK.

A shortcut on the Desktop can be a convenient way of running a program that you use regularly. When new programs are installed, you are sometimes given the option of adding a Desktop shortcut. If not, or you decide later that you want one, you can set up a shortcut in a minute – and if you don't make much use of it, you can remove it even faster!

Sometimes when installing shareware or freeware programs downloaded from the web, Start menu or Desktop shortcuts are not created automatically, and you will have to do it yourself. It's not difficult.

Creating Desktop shortcuts

1 Minimise windows, or move them out of the way so that there is clear Desktop around the Start menu area.

2 Open the Start menu and find the program's entry.

3 Holding down the right mouse button, drag the entry onto the Desktop. You will see a 'ghost' icon with a 'Create link in Desktop' label.

4 Release the mouse button.

5 Select Create shortcut here.

6 Edit the name if necessary.

9

Timesaver tip

You can also create desktop shortcuts to files or folders, so that you can open them with a single click. Just right-click on them in Explorer and select Send To, Desktop.

Creating Desktop shortcuts (cont.)

Jargon buster

Shareware program – a program supplied on a try-before-you-buy basis. At the end of the trial period, you can continue to use the program for a small fee, typically £10 to £20. Shareware programs include the excellent WinZIP file compression software, and Paint Shop Pro, a fully-equipped image editing and creation package.

Jargon buster

Freeware – software ranging from well-meaning efforts of amateurs through to highly professional products like Adobe Reader, which is given away so that people can view the documents and files created by paid-for applications. See pages 70–71 in Chapter 3 for more on these.

The Desktop can get cluttered with all these shortcuts, but it's simple enough to tidy it up. You can change the icon sizes, arrange them in different ways and turn them off altogether if you want a clear Desktop for any reason.

If you don't expect to ever use a shortcut again, select it and press Delete. Note that this only removes the shortcut, not the program, file or folder.

1 Right-click anywhere on the Desktop, point to View and select the icon size.

2 Right-click and point to View again, then tick Align icons to Grid to have the icons arranged in neat lines, and tick Auto Arrange icons if you want the system to tidy them up.

3 Right-click and point to Sort by.

4 Select the property that you want to sort by.

To hide the icons

5 Right-click and point to View, then clear the tick by Show Desktop icons.

9

Customising the Taskbar

The Taskbar is a key part of the control system, offering the simplest way to switch between open windows and to start your most used programs. Customise your Taskbar to suit the way you work. You can adjust the size of the menu icons, turn the clock on or off, hide the Taskbar, or place it on any edge of the screen.

1. Right-click on any blank area of the Taskbar.

2. Select Properties from the context menu.

3. Set the options. Lock the Taskbar fixes its width and position on the screen (see page 241).

4. Auto-hide slides the Taskbar off-screen when not in use. Point off-screen to restore the Taskbar to view.

5. Small icons give you space for more buttons on the Taskbar if you like to run a lot of things at once, but bigger ones are easier to recognise.

6. You can change the Taskbar location – see page 241.

7. The Taskbar buttons can have labels – and these can be useful while you are still learning the icons – and if you have several copies of the same window open at once, the buttons can be combined to save space.

8. Click Apply to see how your settings look – change them if you don't like the effect.

9. Click OK to fix your settings.

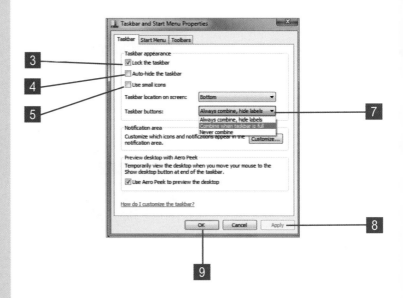

Moving the Taskbar is quite easy to do by mistake, so it is just as well to know how to do it intentionally – if only to correct a mistake!

Resizing the Taskbar – making it deeper or wider – is sometimes useful. Narrow vertical displays are almost unreadable. When you are running a lot of programs with a horizontal Taskbar, the titles on the buttons can be very small. If you deepen the display, you get two rows of decent-sized buttons.

To move the Taskbar

1 In the Taskbar Properties dialogue box, click the Taskbar location button and select the edge – Top, Bottom, Left or Right.

or

2 In the Taskbar Properties dialogue box, clear the Lock the taskbar checkbox, then...

3 Point to any free space on the Taskbar.

4 Drag towards the top, left or right of the screen, as desired.

5 Release the mouse button.

To resize the Taskbar

6 Point to the inside edge of the Taskbar.

7 When the cursor changes to ↔ , drag to change the width of the Taskbar.

Timesaver tip

If you like to keep the Taskbar visible, it takes least space at the top or bottom of the screen.

If you have a lot of applications running at once, or several toolbars on the Taskbar, then the Taskbar is best at the left or right edge, but with Auto-Hide turned on.

Using Taskbar toolbars

To add a toolbar

1 Right-click on an empty place on the Taskbar to open its context menu.

2 Point to Toolbars.

3 Click on a toolbar to add it to (or remove it from) the Taskbar.

To set toolbar options

4 If you right-click over the Notification area, the menu will have a Customise notification icons option. Clicking this will open a window where you can set which icons should be shown, and when. The settings here are really best left at their defaults until you have plenty of experience.

Taskbar toolbars are sets of buttons which live on the Taskbar. Normally the Taskbar will have only the Language bar, apart from the buttons for any open applications and the clock.

If you find that you do not use it, this toolbar can be removed, to allow more space for application buttons.

Over on the right of the Taskbar is the Notification area. The icons here relate to the hardware, e.g. your Internet connection, or carry messages from the system, e.g. alerting you to updates that need attention. You can customise this area too.

If you like the Taskbar as a means of starting programs, you can set up new Taskbar toolbars to hold your own collections of shortcuts to programs that you use regularly.

1 In Windows Explorer, create a new folder – it can be in any convenient place on your hard drive.

2 Set up shortcuts to your main programs. The simplest way to do this is to drag them from the Start menu, with the right mouse button held down, then select Create shortcut here.

3 Open the Taskbar menu, point to Toolbars and select New Toolbar.

4 Select your new folder.

5 Click Select Folder.

6 Your new toolbar will appear on the right of the Taskbar. Click on the double chevrons to open up its list of shortcuts.

9

Creating a user account

1 Click on the User Accounts and Family Safety link in the Control Panel.

2 Select Add or Remove user account.

3 Click Create a new account.

Windows makes it easy for several people to share the use of one PC. Each user can have their own set of folders and their own customised Desktop and Start menu.

There are two types of account:

■ Standard users have access to only their own files and those in the Shared Documents folder. They can customise their own desktops, and decide their own passwords and the pictures which identify their account.
■ Administrators have full access to all aspects of the PC – including other users' areas.

You must have Administrator access to create accounts.

4 Enter the user's name and
click Next.

5 Set the account type.

6 Click Create Account.

Timesaver tip

Click Change the way users
log on and off, and make
sure that Fast User
Switching is enabled.

9

Important

Some older Windows
software may not run
properly with the Standard
account. Users who need
to run such applications
must be set as
Administrators.

Changing user details

Standard users can change only two aspects of their accounts: the password and the picture which appears on the welcome screen and Start menu. Administrator users can change all aspects of their own – or any other user's – account, including the account type. Changes can be made at any time.

1 Click the User Accounts and Family Safety link in the Control Panel. Administrators now need to pick the account.

To change the picture

2 Click Change your picture.

3 Select an image from the offered set or click Browse for more pictures to use one of your own files.

4 Click Change Picture.

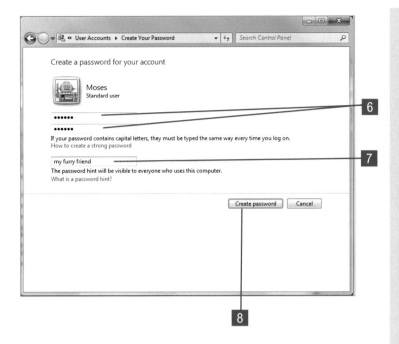

To add a password

5 Click Create a password for your account.

6 Enter the password twice – as you won't be able to read it, this is to check that you have typed it correctly.

7 Enter a hint to help you remember the password.

8 Click Create Password.

Important

Passwords can be a pain and should only be created if needed. If you do create one, click the Prevent a forgotten password link in the Related Tasks and create a 'password reset' disk. This will enable you to recover all your data should you later forget the password.

The password can be anything, but should be something that you can remember but that others are unlikely to guess. And the password hint should not be too obvious – it can be seen by other users.

Jargon buster

.NET Passports – proof of identity that is accepted at many Internet sites that use secure systems to protect confidential data – set one up from here if you find that you need one.

9

Using the Character Map

This shows the full set of characters that are present in any given font, and allows you to select one or more individual characters for copying into other applications. Its main use is probably for picking up Wingdings for decoration, or the odd foreign letter or mathematical symbol in otherwise straight text.

The characters are rather small, but you can get a better look at a character by holding the mouse button down while you point at it. This produces an enlarged image.

1 On the Start menu, select All Programs then go to the Accessories menu, open the System Tools group and select Character Map.

2 Select the Font.

3 Click on a character to highlight it.

4 Click Select to place it into Characters to Copy.

5 Go back over Steps 3 and 4 as necessary.

6 Click Copy to copy to the Clipboard.

7 Return to your application and Paste the characters into it.

Did you know?

In Word, you can insert special characters directly using the Insert Symbol routine.

Gadgets are mini-applications that you can run in the Sidebar, on the right of your Desktop. Some are handy utilities, some show the latest news headlines, stock reports or weather forecasts from the Web, others are just for fun. All are worth exploring.

There are around a dozen gadgets supplied as part of the Windows 7 package, and more available online. These can be added at any time – and removed again if you find that you do not use them.

1 Right-click anywhere on the screen.

2 Select Gadgets.

3 At the gadgets window, right-click on a gadget and select Add.

9

Customising gadgets

Gadgets can be customised and/or controlled, but in different ways, depending upon what they are. Here is the clock, for example. You can change the face, name and the time zone. (You can have several clocks, each set to a different time zone, in which case the name could identify the location.)

1 Point to the top right to get the toolbar and click the Options button – the Clock options dialogue box will appear.

2 Use the arrows to cycle through the choice of faces until you find the one you prefer.

3 If you have several clocks, type in a name to suit the location.

4 Select a time zone.

5 Tick the Show the second hand box, if it is wanted.

6 Click OK.

Important

All gadgets have a mini-toolbar which appears when you point to the top right. It has three parts: a Close button, an Options button and a Handle which is used for moving it.

Close
Options
Handle

The control options apply to all gadgets. Right-click on a gadget to display its menu of controls.

There are only half a dozen.

- Add Gadgets opens the Gadgets Gallery as we saw earlier.

- Move – selects the gadget so that you can move it within the Sidebar. To move it, drag on the handle.

- Size – some gadgets have Small and Large display options.

- Always on top – sets the gadget to display on top of any other windows which may be open. If you turn this on for a gadget, you might want to reduce its opacity.

- Opacity – gadgets can be distracting. If you reduce their opacity and make them more transparent, they are less eye-catching. When you point to one, it becomes solid once more.

- Options opens the Options dialogue box.

- Close Gadget removes the gadget from the Sidebar.

Did you know?

If you have an always-on broadband connection, the Feed Headlines gadget will bring up to the minute news to your desktop.

9

Looking after your PC

Introduction

A modern PC requires very little maintenance – and certainly very little physical maintenance. Wiping the screen with an anti-static cloth from time to time is about all that is normally necessary – if any component fails, there's little you could have done to prevent it, and nothing you can do to mend it (though replacement of most parts is very simple).

It's the hard disk, or rather, the data that is stored on the hard disk, which needs the maintenance. The more a disk is used, and the more data that is stored on it, the more necessary maintenance becomes. Look after your storage, and you should be able to enjoy many years of happy computing; neglect it, and one day you will find that some of your files have gone missing or become unreadable, and they may be essential and irreplaceable.

In this chapter you will learn how to keep your hard disk working efficiently, and how to back up files so that if the worst does happen and your hard disk fails, at least your data will be safe.

What you'll do

Find the System Tools

Check a disk for errors

Defragment a disk

Back up

Restore files from backups

Restore to a previous version

Clean up the hard disk

Remove programs

Change Windows components

Keep Windows up to date

Add a printer

Cancel a print job

Finding the
system tools

1 Click Start.

2 Select Control Panel.

3 Select System and Security.

4 Click on a link to start a job.

These programs will help to keep your disks in good condition, and your data safe.

- Backup – enables you to keep safe copies of your important files, and to recover lost data.
- System Restore – backs up essential files, so that the system can be restored to normal after a crash.
- Disk Cleanup – finds and removes unused files.
- Disk Defragmenter – optimises the organisation of storage to maximise the disk's speed and efficiency.
- Error-check – finds and fixes errors in data stored on disks.
- Scheduled Tasks – lets you perform maintenance at set times.
- System Information – gives (technical) information about what's going on inside your computer.

Most of the tools can be started from the System and Security part of the Control Panel; some are reached through the hard disk's Properties panel.

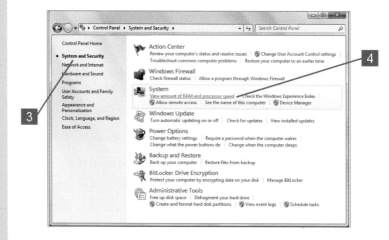

The four system tools that are needed for the routine housekeeping can also be reached from the Properties box of any disk. The messages will remind you of chores you have been neglecting!

1 Open Explorer, right-click on the drive for the context menu.

2 Select Properties.

3 Click Disk Cleanup.

or

4 Go to the Tools tab to start the Error-check, Defragmenter or Backup.

10

Checking a disk for errors

Data is stored on disks in *allocation units*. A small file may fit on a single unit, but others are spread over many. A file's units may be in a continuous run or scattered over the disk (see opposite), but they are all kept together by links from one to the next. Sometimes the links get corrupted leaving *lost fragments*, with no known links to any file, or *cross-linked files*, where two are chained to the same unit of data.

The magnetic surface of the disk may also (rarely) become corrupted, creating *bad sectors* where data cannot be stored.

The Error-checking routine can identify these and, with a bit of luck, retrieve any data written there and transfer it to a safe part of the disk. It is very simple to run, with only two options at the start, and nothing for you to do once it's running.

1. Go to the Tools tab of the disk's Properties dialogue box and click Check Now.
2. For a quick check, turn off the options.
3. If you think the disk has errors, turn on one or other option.
4. Click Start.

- With Automatically fix file system errors on, it will try to solve any problems that it meets – and it will do this better than you or I could, so leave it to it!
- Scan for and attempt recovery of bad sectors will test the surface of the disk, to make sure that files can be stored safely, and rebuild it if necessary. This automatically runs the first option.

If no option is set, the routine simply checks that the files are stored safely.

Important !

Windows cannot check the C: drive while it is being used. If you start an error check on this drive, you will be asked if you want to run a check at the next start up. Click Schedule disk check if you do.

256

When you first start to write data onto a disk, the files are stored one after the other, with each occupying a continuous run of disk space. When you access one of these files, the drive simply finds the start point, then reads the data in a single sweep.

After the disk has been in use for some time, holes begin to appear in the layout, and not all files are stored in a continuous area. Some have been deleted, others will have grown during editing, so that they no longer fit in their original slot, but now have parts stored elsewhere on the disk. When you store a new file, there may not be a single space large enough for it, and it is stored in scattered sections. The drive is becoming *fragmented*. The data is still safe, but the access speed will suffer as the drive now has to hunt for each fragment of the file.

Disk Defragmenter should be run from time to time to pull scattered files together, so that they are stored in continuous blocks. It is best done on a regular schedule, at a time when the PC is not in use.

 Defragmenting a disk

1 Run the Disk Defragmenter from the Control Panel or the disk's Properties box.

2 Click Configure schedule to set the time and frequency.

or

3 Click Analyse disk to see the state of your disk.

4 If the analysis shows it is necessary, click Defragment disk to start the operation.

Important

Defragmenting can take a while and will be even slower if you are using the PC at the time.

10

Backing up ▶

1 Make sure that your external hard drive is connected, if you are using one.

2 On the Tools tab of the disk's Properties panel, click Backup Now... to run Backup Status and Configuration.

3 Click the Set up backup link.

If program files are accidentally deleted, it is a nuisance but not a major problem as you can reinstall the application from the original disks. Data files are different. How much is your data worth to you? How long would it take you to rewrite that report or re-edit that image? Individual files can be copied onto disks for safekeeping, but if you have more than one or two it is simpler to use Backup. A backup job is easily set up and will more than pay for itself in time and effort if you ever need it!

You cannot run a scheduled backup to a removable CD/DVD disk. It must be either to a hard drive elsewhere on the network or to an external hard drive or tape backup device. External hard drives are convenient and cheap – typically well under £100.

The Backup routine is easy to use. To set it up, you specify the storage medium, types of files to be stored and the schedule. The first time that you run it, it will perform a complete backup of all the selected file types; in later backups, it will store only those that are new or have been changed.

4 Select where the backup is to be stored. Notice that you can save on another PC if you are on a network. This may be convenient but is only really safe if the backup PC is in a different building.

5 You can let Windows choose what to backup or pick the folders yourself. It really is best to leave it to Windows unless you are an experienced user and have special requirements.

6 At the Review stage, click Change schedule.

7 Set the schedule, specifying how often, what day and what time. Backing up does not generally take that long, and is not that intrusive, but it will be done faster and more efficiently if you are not using the PC at the time.

8 Click Save settings and exit.

10

Restoring files from backups

With any luck this will never be necessary! But if you need to, it's a simple job.

1 Make sure that your external hard drive is connected, if you are using one.

2 Open the Control Panel, go to System and Security and select Restore files from backup.

3 Choose which files to restore – yours or those of all users.

4 Click Search to hunt for files or files by name.

or

5 Click Browse for files to restore individual files.

or

6 Click Browse for folders to restore entire folders.

7 Locate the files/folders and click Add.

Restoring files from backups (cont.)

8 Restore to its original location if you want to replace the existing files with ones from the backup.

or

9 Select a new location if you want to retain the current versions as well – there may be valuable data in the new files.

10 Click Restore to start the process.

11 If you are restoring to the original location, and there is already a version of the file, you will be asked if you want to replace it.

10

Restoring to a previous version

Even if you don't back up your files, Windows does. It automatically keeps 'shadow copies' of your files and folders as part of the system protection, and you can use these to revert to previous versions of files.

1 Run Windows Explorer and locate the file or folder that you want to recover. Right-click and select Properties from the context menu.

2 At the Properties panel, switch to the Previous Versions tab.

3 Find and select the copy from the last time when the file or folder was in the state you want it to be.

You have three choices:

4 Click Open to open a file for reading and resaving, or open a folder so that files can be selected for recovery.

or

5 Click Copy to copy the file or folder to a new location.

or

6 Click Restore to replace the original file or folder with the shadow copy.

Disk Cleanup is a neat little utility, and well worth running regularly – especially if you spend much time on the Internet. When you are surfing, your browser stores the files for the text, graphics and programs on the web pages that you visit. This makes sense, as it means that if you go back to a page (either in the same session or at a later date), the browser can redraw it from the files, rather than having to download the whole lot again. However, if you don't revisit sites much, you can build up a lot of unwanted clutter on your disk. You can empty this cache from within your browser, but Cleanup will also do it.

The Recycle Bin can be emptied directly, or as part of the Cleanup.

Programs often create temporary files, but do not always remove them. Cleanup will also tidy up after them.

 Cleaning up the hard disk

1 Click Disk Cleanup on the disk's Properties panel.

2 After it has checked the system, the Cleanup panel opens. Select the areas to be cleaned.

3 Click OK.

Important

Administrative users can clean up all the files on the computer. Standard users can only clean up their own areas.

10

See also

If you really want to create some extra space on your system, check through your programs and the Windows Setup and remove any that you do not use. The More Options panel leads to the Add/Remove Programs routine – see the next page for more on this.

Removing Programs

Installing new applications is easy nowadays – you just put the CD in the drive and follow the instructions! Removing unused programs is also easy – but you must do it properly, and not simply delete the application's folder in Windows Explorer. When applications are installed, entries are created in the Start menu, and files are associated with them. These all need to be removed as well. The Uninstall Programs routine will take care of all of this for you.

1 Open the Control Panel, select Programs then Uninstall a program.

2 Select the program.

3 Click Uninstall.

4 You may be asked to confirm the removal of files that may be used by other programs – if in doubt, keep them.

5 Click OK.

Important

If data files have been stored in the program's folder, the routine will not be able to remove them – use Computer/Windows Explorer to tidy up any remnants.

Unwanted parts of Windows 7 can also be removed – and you can add accessories that were omitted during the initial installation.

1 Open the Control Panel, select Programs then Turn Windows features on or off.

2 To remove an entire set of components, click on the checkbox to clear it.

3 To remove part of a set, click ⊞ to open the folder then clear individual check boxes.

4 When you have finished, click OK, wait while Windows reconfigures. It will take a few moments.

Timesaver tip

To add new accessories or other features, tick the checkboxes instead of clearing them!

10

Keeping Windows up to date

Microsoft regularly produces improvements and bug-fixes for Windows, distributing them through the Internet. Windows has an Automatic Updates routine, which can connect regularly to Microsoft's site to get the latest patches and additions.

The Automatic Updates settings can be changed through the System and Security item in the Control Panel. It can:

- Download automatically, notifying you when the files are ready to be installed.
- Alert you if it finds any new critical or optional updates.
- Be turned off completely, if you prefer to use the Windows Update link to check the site when it suits you.

1 Open the Control Panel and select System and Security.

2 Select Windows Update.

To install updates manually

3 If you have chosen to control which updates are installed, and when, you will be told if updates are available. (You must be online so that the Update service can check the Microsoft website.) Click the links to available updates.

4 Clear the checkboxes for any updates that are not relevant to your PC.

5 Click OK.

To change your update settings

6 At the Windows Update window, select Change settings.

7 Select Install automatically, Download updates or Check for updates – you really should update one way or the other.

8 If you opt for automatic update, set the day and time to run the update.

9 Click OK.

! Important

After the files have been downloaded and installed, you normally have to restart the PC to bring them into play, but it doesn't have to be done immediately – finish your session as usual. At the next start up, there will probably be a delay while your system files are updated.

10

Adding a printer

If your printer is not detected and installed automatically by the plug and play technology, you can add it yourself easily. There is a wizard to take you through the steps, and Windows 7 has drivers for almost all but the most recent printers. If you have a very new machine, use the drivers on the printer's setup disk.

1. Open the Control Panel and select View devices and printers in the Hardware and Sound section.

2. Click Add a printer on the toolbar to start the routine.

3. On a home machine, the printer is probably attached to your PC, so select Local.

4. Select the Port – normally LPT1.

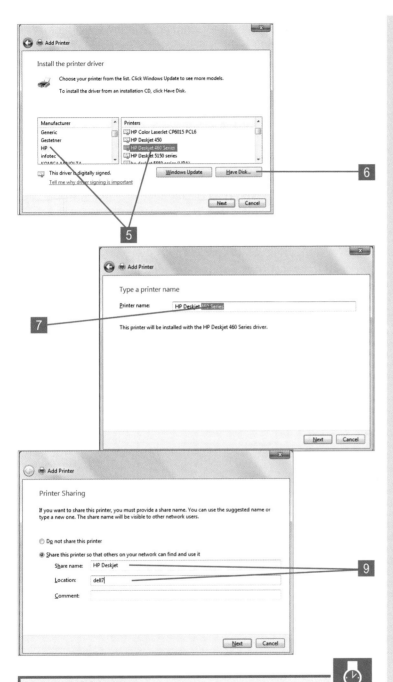

Adding a printer (cont.)

5 Pick the Manufacturer then the Printer from the lists.

or

6 Insert a disk with the printer driver and click Have Disk.

7 Change the name if you like – a networked printer should have a clear recognisable name to identify it.

8 At the final stage opt for the test print, then click Finish and wait.

9 If the printer is to be shared over the local network, give it a Share name and Location so that people can find it easily.

Jargon buster

Drivers – software that converts the formatting information from an application into the right codes for the printer.

10

Timesaver tip

Sometimes the printer problem is obvious – it's run out of paper or ink. If you do not know what the problem is, run the Troubleshooter – this will help you to identify the cause.

Cancelling a print job

1. Open the Printers folder from the Control Panel, right-click on the active printer and select Open.

   or

2. Right-click on the 🖶 icon in the Taskbar and select the printer.

3. Select the file(s).

4. Press Delete or open the Document menu and select Cancel.

When you send a document for printing, Windows will happily handle it in the background. It prepares the file for the printer, stores it in a queue if the printer is already busy or offline, pushes the pages out one at a time and deletes the temporary files it has created. Nothing visible happens on screen – unless the printer runs out of paper or has other faults.

This is fine when things run smoothly, but they don't always when you are printing. You may run out of ink or paper part way through the job; you may decide that you don't like the look of the first page of a long document so that there is no point in printing the rest; and sometimes your PC and your printer will get their wires crossed for no discernable reason. If you need to cancel the printing of a document, it can be done.

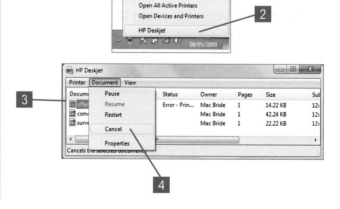

Jargon buster

Branch – in file management, the structure of sub-folders that opens off from a folder.

Browser – application specially designed for accessing and displaying the information in the World Wide Web. This is also true the other way: the web is an information system designed to be viewed on browsers.

Child folder – in file management, a sub-folder of a Parent.

Clipboard – Windows has a special part of memory known as the Clipboard, which can be used for storing any kind of data – text, images, spreadsheets, complete files or small selected chunks. It can be used not just for copying or moving data within an application, but also between applications as the Clipboard can be accessed from any program.

Document – Windows uses 'document' to mean any file created by any application. A word-processed report is obviously a document, but so is a picture file from a graphics package, a data file from a spreadsheet, a video clip, sound file – in fact, any file produced by any program.

Driver – software that handles the interaction between the computer and a peripheral device. A printer driver converts the formatting information from an application into the right codes for the printer.

Email – electronic mail, a system for sending messages and files across networks.

Error-checking – the techniques used to make sure that data sent over the Internet arrives intact. If a block of data is damaged, it is sent again.

Freeware – software ranging from well-meaning efforts of amateurs through to highly professional products like Adobe Reader, which is given away so that people can view the documents and files created by paid-for applications.

GUI – Graphical User Interface – the screen display for an operating system such as Windows, that uses images, icons and menus. Users start operations and make choices by clicking on these, rather than having to type in command words.

HTML – HyperText Markup Language, a system of instructions that browsers can interpret to display text and images. HTML allows hypertext links to be built into web pages.

ISP – Internet Service Provider – the company that supplies your connection to the Internet.

Keyword – a keyword can be any word which might occur in the pages that you are looking for. If you give two or more, the system will only list pages which contain all those words.

Mail server – a computer that stores and handles email, either within a large organisation or at an ISP.

Net – short for Internet. And Internet is short for interlinked networks, which is what it is.

.Net passports – proof of identity that is accepted at many internet sites that use secure systems to protect confidential data – set one up from the User Accounts facility if you find that you need one.

Page – or web page, a document displayed on the web. It may be plain or formatted text; and may hold pictures, sounds and videos.

Parent folder – in file management, a folder that contains another.

Plain text – text without any layout or font formatting.

Root – in file management, the folder of the disk. All other folders branch off from the root.

Shareware program – a program supplied on a try-before-you-buy basis. At the end of the trial period, you can continue to use the program for a small fee, typically £10 to £20. Shareware programs include the excellent WinZIP file compression software, and Paint Shop Pro, a fully-equipped image editing and creation package.

Snail mail – mail that is hand-delivered by the postman.

Template – document that has formatting and layout in place ready for your text. It may have some text and images in place already, e.g. headed paper for letters.

Web – the World Wide Web, also shortened to WWW or W3.

Troubleshooting guide

Basic Windows

Customising Windows

Editing and printing in Word

Email

File management

Formatting text

Getting Help

Graphics

Housekeeping

PC hardware

The Internet

Working with text

New! Features

Microsoft Windows 7

Microsoft Windows 7 is the fastest and most reliable version of Windows yet. It provides closer integration of the Desktop with online services through the Windows Live programs and web sites; new 'libraries' for organising files and folders; an Office-style Ribbon interface for Windows accessories and many more improvements to the interface and underlying processes.

What's New?

The **New!** icon in the table of contents highlights the sections that have been significantly revised. The following lists all the significantly revised and new sections and their location in the book.